healing worship
PURPOSE &
PRACTICE

Bruce G. Epperly

The Pilgrim Press
Cleveland

The Pilgrim Press
700 Prospect Avenue
Cleveland, Ohio 44115-1100
thepilgrimpress.com
© 2006 by Bruce G. Epperly

Scripture quotations, unless otherwise noted, are from the New Revised
Standard Version of the Bible, © 1989 by the Division of Christian Education of
the National Council of Churches of Christ in the United States of America and
are used by permission. Changes have been made for inclusivity.

Printed in the United States of America on acid-free paper

10 09 08 07 06   5 4 3 2 1

Library of Congress Cataloging-in-Publication Data

Epperly, Bruce Gordon.
    Healing worship / Bruce G. Epperly.
       p. cm.
    Includes bibliographical references.
    ISBN-13: 978-0-8298-1742-3
    1. Spiritual healing. 2. Healing—Religious aspects—Christianity. I. Title.
BT732.5.E67 2006
234'.131—dc22   2006019990
ISBN-13: 978-0-8298-1742-3
ISBN-10: 0-8298-1742-5

Contents

chapter one

Healing Without Supernaturalism

Now there was a woman who had been suffering from hemorrhages for twelve years. She had endured much under many physicians, and had spent all that she had; and she was no better, but rather grew worse. She had heard about Jesus, and came up behind him in the crowd, and touched his cloak, for she said, "If I but touch his clothes, I will be made well." Immediately her hemorrhage stopped; and she felt in her body that she was healed of her disease. Immediately aware that power had gone forth from him, Jesus turned about in the crowd and said, "Who touched my clothes?" And his disciples said to him, "You see the crowd pressing in on you; how can you say, 'Who touched me?'" He looked all around to see who had done it. But the woman, knowing what had happened to her, came in fear and trembling, fell down before him, and told him the whole truth. He said to her, "Daughter, your faith has made you well; go in peace; and be healed of your disease." (Mark 5:25–34)

NEW HORIZONS OF HEALING

Each Wednesday evening at her congregation's healing service, Rev. Susan Frey looks out at the small group of regulars who gather week after week in the sanctuary chancel for prayer and support. Although she knows their most obvious physical and spiritual challenges, Rev. Frey often wonders what really brings her parishioners to this intimate time of silence, scripture, prayer, and laying on of hands. "Why do they show up every week, while the majority of the congregation, including some with more serious health issues, absent themselves from this time of healing prayer? What makes these people unique in my congregation? What keeps them coming despite the fact there are only occasional signs of physical or emotional improvement?"

As each participant enters the sanctuary, Rev. Frey prayerfully asks herself, "How can I respond to their quest for healing through worship and pastoral care? Frankly, how can I address the many other unspoken cries for healing in my congregation?"

Over the years, Rev. Frey has come to know the challenges that face the regular participants in this intimate healing circle. She has heard their stories, touched them in prayer, visited them in the hospital, and anointed them with oil in the name of the healer Jesus Christ. This evening, as she looks out at the faithful dozen who come in search of divine healing, she takes a moment to reflect on a few of their stories.[1]

Like the woman described in Mark's gospel, Suzanne has lived patiently with chronic pain and weakness for nearly a decade. Although she has gone from physician to physician and explored complementary approaches to health care, Suzanne struggles just to make it through the day. Still, she searches for a miracle—a return to effortless physical activity and overall well-being that will allow her to work a full day, volunteer at the soup kitchen, and play with her three grandchildren. "I'm looking for a miracle cure," Suzanne confesses, "but now I know that the miracle I really need may be different from the one I'm seeking. I'm learning to believe that in all things, God is working for good, and that includes my pain. This may be the real miracle!"

At fifty-five, Larry is facing a medical death sentence—the prognosis of surviving liver cancer for more than a few years is less than fifty-fifty. Like Suzanne, he combines Western medicine with complementary health care and spiritual direction. His multi-disciplinary approach has reduced his symptoms and given him a sense of personal empowerment as he faces the likelihood of death. Though he also prays for a miracle cure, realistically he hopes for a gentle and painless death at home in the company of his friends and family. Larry believes that he has already received a profound spiritual healing—he is no longer afraid of the debilitation and death that are his likely prognosis. In his own understated way, he asserts, "Now I know the meaning of Psalm 23. Even though I am walking in the valley of the shadow of death right now, I'm not afraid anymore. I know that God is with me. I have felt God's presence and comfort when everything else had failed me. I know that whatever happens, God will remain beside me and that someday I will dwell in God's house forevermore."

Anita prays each week for strength to deal creatively with her mother's Alzheimer's disease. Nearly at the end of her financial and emotional resources, Anita knows that soon she will no longer be able to care for her mother at home. But institutionalization seems like a failure of love and a betrayal of her mother's unspoken trust. She prays for the wisdom to make the right decision for her mother, and the patience and love to embrace someone who now barely recognizes her. She also prays that she might be able to accept and forgive herself for her limitations as a daughter and caregiver. "I find acceptance and forgiveness in the healing service. I am learning that God loves me in spite of my limitations and imperfections and that God has a plan for us that cannot be thwarted by Alzheimer's disease. Going to the service is like taking medicine. Each time I attend, I feel greater acceptance and strength, and this helps me deal with my doubts and struggles in the week ahead."

Like the others who come week after week to the mid-week healing service, these three have *not* fully experienced the cures for which they initially prayed. Indeed, among the core membership of the healing service, three members have died of cancer in the past year. But, still the regulars—and a few newcomers—come each week, hoping to experience the touch of God that will transform their lives and bring wholeness to their families. Some of the regulars no longer expect a physical cure, but simply pray to respond creatively to conditions beyond their control. Virtually everyone at the service can claim to have experienced a spiritual healing, reflected in a greater sense of God's presence and support amid the storms of life. The few who have experienced physical cures have also sought the aid of Western and complementary health care givers. Still, they affirm that healing prayers and laying on of hands were as important in restoring their health as were medications, surgery, or complementary care.

Rev. Frey struggles each week to speak a healing word to her small mid-week congregation. She knows that many of them have been hurt by thoughtless relatives who piously proclaimed, "If you only have more faith, you will get well," or, "If you only go to a spirit-filled church, you will receive a miracle." She knows that these voices echo in their minds and hearts and that she must be careful not to raise old wounds by a poorly chosen word or an inept expression of a theological concept. For her Wednesday evening healing circle, the abstract theological term "theodicy" becomes a lived experience as members ask themselves, "What did I do wrong to bring this on my child?" "Am I being punished for some youthful indiscretion?" "Where is God's love in the pain I feel?"

Often, participants question their own faith after viewing the dramatic, and often carefully choreographed, healings presented by televangelists. "Why don't these dramatic manifestations of divine power happen at our church? What's wrong with our faith and theology? Do I need to speak in tongues for the Holy Spirit to cure my cancer or my friend's depression?" Rev. Frey knows that these questions weigh heavily not only on the participants in the Wednesday evening healing service, but also on those who choose not to attend despite their physical, emotional, or relational challenges. She knows that the faith that lures some to the congregation's healing service repels others who see healing prayer as a gimmick or placebo, a trick to fool the simpleminded, or a denial of the realities of sickness and death. Nevertheless, week after week for the past several years, Rev. Frey gathers this small circle for prayer, touch, scripture, and fellowship. She knows that, as their pastor, she also needs healing and transformation as she faces her own feelings of inadequacy, struggles to believe in a healing God, and fears that she will inadvertently bring greater pain to persons who have already experienced so much agony and sorrow.

Each Wednesday afternoon as Rev. Frey prepares her evening homily and goes over the order of worship, she prays that the service will truly be *healing worship*. She also prays that her vocation as pastor will truly become a *healing ministry*, and that her leadership in the Sunday worship services and various board meetings will reflect God's desire to heal both persons and institutions.

As she reflects on the history of the midweek healing service, Rev. Frey ponders the radical changes that have occurred in the relationship between medicine and spirituality over the past twenty years and the growing interest in the healings of Jesus within her critically-thinking mainstream Protestant congregation. The idea of praying for a physical cure or emotional transformation would have been deemed foolish superstition by her rationalist congregation twenty years ago. But ten years ago, when she initiated the healing service in partnership with the leaders of the congregation's Stephen Ministry, there was more curiosity than resistance. As she looks at her own bookshelf and considers the reading habits of her congregation, she notices texts on spirituality and healing by persons as diverse as Larry Dossey, Deepak Chopra, Andrew Weil, Dale Matthews, Christine Northrup, and Harold Koenig.[2] She finds it amusing, yet significant, that physicians and scientists discovered the power of prayer to transform persons' lives before mainstream pastors and church leaders proclaimed the connection of spirituality and health from their pulpits.

Pastor Frey also knows that many members of her congregation are embracing complementary and alternative medicine. Virtually everyone who comes to the healing service has seen at least one complementary health care giver—an acupuncturist, herbalist, massage therapist, reiki or healing touch practitioner, or homeopathic physician—along with the family practitioner and specialists. Their journeys toward healing have been profoundly spiritual in nature, awakening them to Christian and non-Christian spiritual disciplines. Rev. Frey does her best to keep up with the popular literature on healing and wholeness so that she can provide a bridge between Christian faith and complementary medicine for her parishioners.

Rev. Frey believes in "miracles," acts of divine power and transformation, but she cannot theologically affirm the arbitrary supernaturalism taught by many faith healers and televangelists. She believes that God is always at work in the world, although primarily in gentle and undramatic ways. As she reads the breathtaking stories of physical cures touted by televangelists, she sometimes wonders if her own more naturalistic approach to divine activity expects too little from God. As she ponders the story of the woman with the flood of blood, she wonders, "Could it be that our faith will truly make us well if we find a point of contact with God and throw ourselves completely upon God's mercy? Do such events represent a divine intervention suspending the laws of nature or an actualization of universal, but mostly neglected, healing energies that are released by our faith? If God is present in my ministry and congregation, what more can I do in order to mediate God's healing presence to hurting people?"

Today, the healer Jesus has been rediscovered by mainstream and progressive Christians. Biblical scholars as diverse as Marcus Borg and John Meier have recognized that healing was central to Jesus' message and embodiment of God's coming reign.[3] Congregations of widely diverse denominational and theological perspectives have initiated health ministries, parish nursing programs, and healing services. Still, many mainstream and progressive congregations struggle to maintain their healing services or integrate healing prayer into their Sunday services. What began with anticipation and excitement often fades into oblivion through diminished interest and attendance. Many pastors, such as Rev. Frey, wonder why the healing service remains at the periphery of congregational life, an appendage rather than a major emphasis of the congregation's overall ministry. They believe that an emphasis on God's desire for healing and shalom should be at the heart of the total ministry of the church, embracing and enlivening its ministries of worship, education, service, and outreach as well as its specific congregational health and healing ministries. These pastors and congregational leaders are searching for a constructive theology of healing and integrative forms of worship and spiritual practices that will undergird their congregations' healing services.[4]

HEALING THEOLOGY

Theology has a bad reputation among many Christians. On the one hand, many pastors and laypersons see the language of theology as abstract, incomprehensible, and irrelevant to their daily lives. In their minds, theological doctrines and controversies have virtually no practical application in the life of the church. On the other hand, they recognize that many traditional theological doctrines, especially those that relate to health, sickness, and disability, often do more harm than good for persons in need of spiritual and physical healing.

If healing services are to find their rightful place in the church, they need to be grounded in the integration of theological reflection and spiritual formation. As theologian Abigail Rian Evans affirms, "The preparation and education before these services is also crucial. This educational prelude is almost as important as the services themselves."[5]

I believe that such theological reflection is essential to the overall health of the church and its members. Healthy theology promotes personal and corporate well-being, while toxic theology leaves in its wake feelings of guilt, hopelessness, and impotence. In certain cases, our theological beliefs can be the tipping point between health and illness, and life and death. With Evans, I believe that "healing liturgies have, on occasion, been based on a misapplication of the theology of miraculous healing, as well as the inappropriate exclusion of medical means and other health resources."[6] While the theologian's primary task is to present lively, constructive, and biblically-grounded visions of God and human life, the theologian—like the physician—must, first, "do no harm" in her or his expression of the Christian faith. The constructive task of practical theology also involves challenging doctrines that undermine our confidence in God's graceful, healing presence in our lives.

Jesus was a practical theologian, whose words were embodied in acts of healing and liberation. When Jesus encountered a man who had been blind from birth, his disciples asked, "Who sinned, this man or his parents, that he was born blind?" In response, Jesus presented a healing vision in word and deed by questioning the popular and seldom questioned theology of his own time (John 9:1–7). First, Jesus denied a linear cause and effect—rewards and punishments—relationship between sin and sickness. Jesus implicitly affirmed that God seeks well being for all humankind in the context of the realities of sickness, sin, and injustice. Accidents happen to the faithful and unfaithful alike—"[God] makes [God's] sun to rise on the evil and on the good, and sends rain on the righteous and on the unrighteous" (Matthew 5:45). Jesus asserted that the man's blindness was not due to his parents' unrighteousness or the man's own prenatal sinfulness, but the result of factors beyond the control of both parent and child (John 9:3). Second, this healing story demonstrates Jesus' desire to mediate by his touch God's abundant life to all persons, even those suffering from chronic disabilities. In the spirit of the Hebraic prophets, Jesus affirmed that God has a bias toward shalom—health and wholeness—in the lives of persons and institutions.

In this healing encounter, Jesus did not enter into an extended theological discussion. He simply employed an everyday folk remedy to activate God's ever-present healing energy, and then challenged his own followers to be healing partners while God's light is still available to them. Jesus' healing ministry reminds us that divine healing arises not only from the interplay of our faith and God's desire for healing, but also from our appropriate use of a variety of complementary and Western medicines.

Healthy theology is, above all, practical. It presents an integrative and life-affirming vision of reality; it tells people that they can experience the truths that it asserts; and it provides a pathway to lived experience of theological doctrines. If our minds and bodies are intimately connected, then our theological beliefs *will* make a difference in the health of our cells and organs as well as our overall well-being. As the apostle Paul proclaims, "Do not be conformed to this world, but be transformed by the renewing of your minds" (Romans 12:2). Healthy theology renews and transforms our lives at every level.

In formulating a constructive theology of healing in this chapter and the next, the healer Jesus will be our guide and inspiration. While Jesus did not claim to be a systematic theologian, his words and deeds provide the foundation for a healing theology for our time. The healer from Nazareth set the stage for his future ministry with his interpretation of the prophet Isaiah:

The Spirit of the Lord is upon me, because he has anointed me to bring good news to the poor. He has sent me to proclaim release to the captives and recovery of sight to the blind, to let

the oppressed go free, to proclaim the year of the Lord's favor.
(Luke 4:18–19)

Jesus' affirmation that "I came that they might have life, and
have it abundantly" includes every dimension of life (John
10:10). When John the Baptist sends his disciples to ask Jesus if
he is the Messiah, he responds:

Go and tell John what you have seen and heard: the blind
receive their sight, the lame walk, the lepers are cleansed, the
deaf hear, the dead are raised, the poor have good news brought
to them. (Luke 7:22–23)

The first, and most important, task of a healing theology is
to proclaim the good news that God wants us to be healthy and
whole, regardless of our current physical or mental condition.
God does not punish us with cancer, AIDS, heart disease, or
chronic disability. While our actions and attitudes have consequences and may be factors in health or illness, God's desire for
every person and in every situation is healing, without exception. God aims at authentic healing or shalom—the peace of
mind, body, and spirit that comes from the recognition that we
are always in God's hands and, therefore, can always awaken
to new spiritual and relational possibilities in every life situation and health condition. Persons in the final stages of illness
may receive spiritual and emotional healing even though they
do not receive a physical cure. Accordingly, the most important
affirmation that a pastor can give to her or his congregation
and to people facing serious illness or caring for seriously-ill relatives is that "God is on your side and wants you to find health
and wholeness. Jesus came into the world not to condemn or
punish you, but to save and heal you *today*—in this moment—
as well as in the future."

Second, the pastor-theologian's task is to present a biblically-grounded and lively vision of the relationship of divine and

human power working together for healing and wholeness. The woman with the hemorrhage received both a cure and healing as a result of the interplay of her faith and God's universal desire for healing. When Jesus proclaimed, "Your faith has made you well," he was *not* asserting that she was fully responsible for her cure or her previous illness. The cure she experienced was not entirely in her own hands. Rather, her faith opened the door to the release of divine power to transform her life. Her faith was essential but not sufficient to heal her body, mind, spirit, and relationships. A power went forth from Jesus that touched the woman when she reached out to touch him. The scripture suggests that divine power was already present to heal her even apart from Jesus' conscious awareness of the particular manifestations of divine healing that day. Her faith may have been a tipping point among the constellation of factors that were at work in that unique moment of experience.

Healthy theology avoids the two extremes of impotence and omnipotence when it comes to the interplay of divine and human power. On the one hand, God's power as revealed in the healer Jesus is relational rather than coercive. God works within the concreteness of our lives to promote healing and wholeness. In contrast to traditional understandings of divine omnipotence that implicitly assert that everything from cancer to terrorist attacks and tsunamis reflects the inscrutable and inexorable will of God, a healing theology understands divine power primarily in terms of love and creative transformation. Like a good parent, God seeks the well-being of each beloved son and daughter. God does not hurt in order to heal, nor does God interfere with our own evolving creativity and freedom. God wants us to grow in wisdom, stature, and faithfulness, and provides the appropriate conditions for our spiritual and personal growth in light of our personal choices, current health conditions, and the concrete realities of our lives.

Literal and uncritical interpretations of passages such as the healing of the woman with the flow of blood imply that persons are entirely in control of their health and illness. Some persons suggest that the words "your faith has made you well" mean that your sickness and health are entirely in your own hands. They promise that if you have enough faith, you will recover. But, if you do not get well, then you are obviously to blame. "If you only have more faith and make a generous gift to our ministry as a sign of that faith, you will be cured," is the oft-repeated mantra of certain faith healers and popular evangelists. This interpretation of sickness and health, given by many pious believers and television healers, is only slightly different from the popular new age affirmation that "you create your own reality." Focusing on our faith or simply the power of positive thinking denies the interactive roles of God, individuals, and the praying community as factors in the healing process. Further, while healings elicited by such behaviors enhance the public notoriety of faith healers, it is interesting to note these healers rarely admit responsibility for persons whose health conditions remain stable or deteriorate in spite of their heartfelt prayers and contributions to their healing ministries.

A healing theology recognizes that suffering is real and pain can demoralize us. As I tell my seminary and medical students, always listen to a person's description of physical or emotional pain, even if it appears to have no organic basis. While the biblical witness affirms that, in the end, God's healing reign of shalom will be victorious, scripture also asserts that, in the meantime, our experiences of injustice, death, sin, and violence are quite real. This viewpoint provides a stark contrast to the cheery platitudes of some new age pundits, such as best-selling author Wayne Dyer, whose vision of reality has influenced popular understandings of sickness, health, and prosperity.[7] According to Dyer: "You have no problems, though you think you have," and, "If God is good and God made everything, then everything is good."[8] Though we may affirm, with the mystic Julian of Norwich, that "all will be well" in God's ultimate aim for our lives, such over-optimistic spiritual counsel may be destructive for those who have experienced systemic oppression and poverty, sexual abuse, family violence, the death of a child as a result of the actions of a drunk driver, or life with AIDS or cancer. Dyer's counsel to the man born blind would have been for him to recognize that his blindness is a karmic lesson, meant to advance his spiritual journey in this lifetime. His physical blindness is not arbitrary or beyond his control, but reflects the impact of his previous behavior. His physical blindness, as some new age teachers suggest, may be a psychosomatic manifestation of some reality that he refuses to "see."

While we may want to be in control of our lives, the quest for absolute control is bought at the price of blaming yourself or another for whatever illness or negativity we experience. Practically speaking, Dyer's implicit theology—and much new age spirituality—differs little from the doctrine of double predestination held by John Calvin and his more literal followers, except that the locus of power is found in the individual self rather than the omnipotent God. Every moment, such metaphysical views assert, is a perfect moment because it reflects either the will of an omnipotent God, the working out of the soul's destiny, or the unfolding of moral law in the black and white world of sin and punishment. In any case, our pain is an illusion to be minimized or an occasion for overwhelming guilt at the mess we've made of our lives.

Oddly enough, the vision of individualistic omnipotence characteristic of many traditional and contemporary theological positions leads some persons to blame the victims of serious illness, abuse, and poverty, and, ultimately, to withhold both personal and corporate compassion for vulnerable persons who are in greatest need of our love. Listen to the condemnation that lies beneath these popular theological explanations for illness and abuse:

- "After all, it's their fault that they are sick. If they practiced good hygiene or trusted God, they would be healthy."

- "Perhaps she was sending signals to her abuser that she wanted an intimate relationship."
- "The cancer was part of the soul's educational journey. It reflects lessons that they need to learn from their past lives."
- "If they are homeless and out of work, it must be their fault. After all, the real cause of poverty is lack of initiative and a poor work ethic."

In contrast, healthy theology reminds us that in a world of dynamic relationships, we cannot take full credit for our success, nor can we blame ourselves or others entirely for our failures.

Healthy theology must challenge popular understandings of both the omnipotent mind and the omnipotent God. Health and illness are, for the most part, the result of many factors rather than one. While the importance of particular factors varies from person to person, health and illness generally result from the dynamic interplay of factors such as spiritual commitments, attitudes, emotions, life history, relationships, genetics, impact of family of origin, environment and workplace, medical history, and historical events. Environmental catastrophes such as Love Canal, the *Exxon Valdez*, and the depletion of the ozone layer contribute to higher incidents of cancer. Social upheavals, such as the terrorist attacks of September 11, 2001, and fear of future terrorist attacks, raise personal and corporate anxiety and are reflected in our blood pressure and sense of security. Our attitudes may tip the balance between health and illness, but their impact is always shaped by a myriad of factors beyond our personal control.

I believe that theological positions rise and fall on how they respond to the most vulnerable in our midst. How would you explain to the spouse of terrorist victim, a woman sexually abused by her mother, the parent of a child diagnosed with cancer, or a family who lost everything due to Hurricane Katrina that their suffering is entirely the working out of their soul's destiny or God's will in their lives? Only a dynamic, multi-factorial understanding of the causes of health and illness can adequately acknowledge the suffering we experience even as it empowers us to use our own personal and limited freedom to transform the pain of ourselves and others.

Healthy Christian theology asserts that within the many factors of life, there is a gentle force of healing. God works within our health condition, family life, relationships, and social circumstances to bring about healing and wholeness. Biblical theology testifies to the multi-factorial nature of health and illness. Virtually all of the healing stories in the gospels involve a divine-human partnership in the healing process. Divine healing energy is released in dramatic ways through the faith of friends, the love of a parent, the willingness of persons to cross social, ethnic, and political boundaries, and one's personal trust in the healer Jesus despite a lifetime of failure and alienation.

On the social and political level, the biblical tradition affirms that God's relationship with the children of Israel is profoundly dialogical in nature. God works within the context of Israel's fidelity or infidelity to its Creator. Although God's people must face the consequences of idolatry and sin, God does not coerce the people, but seeks redemption even in the most desperate socio-political situations. When Israel is faithful in its praise and ethics, divine protection and healing are more effectively released to transform persons and political communities. Our prayers and fidelity enable God's will to be more fully realized in our lives and in the world. This divine-human synergy is reflected in the words of Hebrew Bible scholar Denise Dombkowski Hopkins:

> When God is praised and praised properly, God is the better for it. God's power is more focused; God's power becomes more magnified because God allows and equips the entire universe to sing divine praises. We praise, not just for the sake of spreading

God's name among the world and among ourselves, but for God's sake as well. If our praise makes a difference for the world, it also makes a difference for God.[9]

The interplay of divine creativity and human response does not insure that diseases will be cured or terrorists disarmed. But it does enable us to be conscious and active partners in God's healing quest to prevent illness and terrorist attacks as well as provide resources to bring healing to the sick and justice to the oppressed. In light of the divine-human healing partnership, the pastor can invite his or her congregation to affirm, "While we are not in complete control of our lives, we can choose to be active partners with God in healing ourselves and the world."

A healthy theology also proclaims that God is truly "the one to whom all hearts are open and all desires known." Taken seriously, this traditional prayer contains one of the most radical Christian affirmations: God's experience and action in the world is shaped, to a significant extent, by our faithfulness and openness to God's presence in our lives. When Jesus affirmed, "Just as you did it to one of the least of these who are members of my family, you did it to me," he proclaimed that what happens in the world truly matters to God (Matthew 25:31–46). Our lives shape God's concrete experience and condition God's response to ourselves and to the world. Our pain and joy are embraced by God. God feels the pain of the mother of a child with cancer, a father struggling with his son's mental illness, a daughter agonizing over her mother's Alzheimer's disease, and thousands of persons displaced by hurricanes and tsunamis. God does not sit aloof on the sidelines of our lives, but is in the midst of our lives—knowing our challenges and successes from the inside. The love of God revealed in the life and ministry of Jesus the healer is not that of a "Saturday parent," who shows up every once in a while with majestic signs and wonders and then leaves the dirty work of life to the custodial spouse; rather, God is an ever-present force whose love is receptive as well as active.

Jesus' own healings were interactive in style. He responded to cries for help in a variety of ways, comforted the sick, and empathetically experienced the grief of widows. Jesus was willing to listen before he acted. "What do you want me to do for you?" he asked one who sought healing for his blindness (Luke 18:35–43). To a man who had been paralyzed for nearly forty years, he asked, "Do you want to be made well?" (John 5:1–9) Jesus had compassion for the sick and outcast regardless of the circumstances that led to their current social and physical condition. In feeling their pain, he was moved to share God's healing touch with them.

I believe that God works in both dramatic and subtle ways throughout our lives. When we awaken to God's presence, "miracles," or acts of divine healing power, burst forth to transform our spirits, relationships, and emotional lives, even if the body remains broken or the healing process takes years to be completed. As with Jesus' own healing ministry, these miracles do not abrogate the laws of nature or dissolve the intricate web of causal relationships. But within the intricate interplay of mind, body, spirit, emotions, and the openness of faith communities, our spiritual practices, attitudes, and healing services may lead to the alleviation of emotional and physical symptoms and, at times, the complete cure of physical ailments.

In a world in which God is the deepest reality of all things, constantly addressing the world in "sighs too deep for words," all moments are, at base, miraculous in nature (Romans 8:26). All moments reveal God's generous aim at abundant life. We can affirm healing without expecting supernatural violations of the predictable processes of nature. As partners in God's universal passion for shalom, we can expect surprising releases of divine energy that transform our bodies, minds, and spirits. The healing pastor can invite her or his congregation to affirm that "God feels our pain and seeks our healing in every life situation and so should we!"

HEALING WORSHIP

Don Saliers describes worship as "primary theology."[10] Our worship reflects and shapes our vision of God, the world, and ourselves, and connects us to the Holy through word, song, movement, and ritual. In the interplay of intercession, praise, and thanksgiving, authentic worship places the totality of our lives in the presence of the healing God. In times of community worship, we practice our faith in words, deeds, hymns, and prayers. Worship truly is an exercise in radical amazement, to paraphrase Rabbi Abraham Joshua Heschel, for the words we use point to the cosmic reality within which we live, move, and have our being. Just randomly open a hymn book and you will discover the wonder and boldness our hymns inspire. Just listen a moment to these imaginative and life-transforming affirmations of faith from traditional hymns of the church:

- God has eternal life implanted in soul. God shall be our strength and stay, while ages roll. ("The God of Abraham Praise")

- Now thank we all our God with heart and mind and voices, who wondrous things has done, in whom the world rejoices, who, from our mother's arms, has blessed us on our way, with countless gifts of love, and still is ours today. ("Now Thank We All Our God")

- There is a balm in Gilead to make the wounded whole, there is a balm in Gilead to heal the sin-sick soul. ("There is a Balm in Gilead")

These same healing affirmations can be found in more contemporary hymns such as: "Precious Lord Take My Hand," "Healer of our Ev'ry Ill," and "He Touched Me."[11] In worship, we—like the aboriginal singers of Australia—describe, shape, and experience a world in which suffering and pain are realities that call us to compassionate action in light of God's ultimate healing of creation. In song and prayer, we are inspired to chart the frontiers of God's love with the recognition that the horizon of healing always lies beyond our wildest dreams. In worship, we pray for things that are unimaginable to those who cannot look beyond the world as it is—justice and peace among the nations, serenity in the storm, healing for the sick and dying, forgiving the enemy—and trust that the One whose praises we sing and guidance we ask will respond with grace and power. We also pray for the "impossible possibility" that God might call us to be partners in healing the world.

Worship is a profound act of trust and imagination. In contrast to the zero-sum, one-dimensional, closed system world views that often characterize our perception of everyday life, the community at worship envisages a world of miracle and surprise in which we expect great things not only of God, but also of ourselves. In this God-permeated world, life is abundant, hope is real, and healing is always on the horizon. We dare to believe Jesus' promise:

Ask, and it will be given you; search, and you will find; knock, and the door will be opened for you . . . [H]ow much more will the heavenly [Parent] give the Holy Spirit to those who ask him! (Luke 11:9, 13b)

For a few hours each week, the community gathers to affirm the holy adventure that calls us to be partners in healing the planet, our loved ones, and ourselves. God's vision of us is always more than we imagine. Jesus promises his disciples then and now that they can do greater things than they can imagine in the healing of body, mind, spirit, and relationships. In healing worship, we dare to believe great things about God and ourselves. We dare to claim that our lives matter in the healing of the world and that our prayers make a difference to God and those we love. Though we do not know what is best for ourselves, our loved ones, and the planet, we humbly plead for the experience of the transformation, healing, and peace that was at the heart of Jesus' healing gospel. As we pray for God's healing touch in the concreteness of our lives, we may ask for God's wisdom in responding to the needs of an aging parent, in deciding the course of medical care for ourselves or a loved one, or in facing the stark reality of death.

Healing worship embraces body, mind, spirit, emotions, relationships, and politics. Liturgies of healing teach us to see the world with new eyes, to touch and be touched in safe and affirming ways, to entertain new and inspiring images of God, and to place both past and future in God's hands. Our prayers do not invoke a distant, otherwise unconcerned deity, but awaken us to God's healing touch within us and around us in each moment of life. The familiar words of praise and prayer and the rituals of touch and anointing join us with God's holy desire for healing and wholeness. The prayers of the faithful focus God's healing energy that is within ourselves and our community on those for whom we pray. In so doing, they help to create a healing environment in which acts of healing power may occur. Our prayers and rituals do not summon an amoral and indifferent God but align us with the Divine Spirit's highest aims for ourselves, the world, and the ones for whom we pray. As Abigail Rian Evans proclaims, "The Spirit of God and the faith of the worshippers gives liturgies their power."[12] Healing worship empowers us to become partners in God's shalom.

The omnipresent God promotes our healing adventures in countless ways. If we choose to be open to God's presence, we discover that all places are God-filled, all moments healing moments, all encounters opportunities for transformation. Accordingly, all worship is meant to be healing, that is, to enlarge our perspective on life, awaken us to untapped spiritual resources, nurture our belief that nothing can separate us from the love of God, and inspire our partnership in God's healing adventure. Every aspect of worship from the sermon to the hymns to the architecture and accessibility of the sanctuary should be aimed at embodying God's shalom in this time and place. Worship services whose primary aim is healing and wholeness are not meant to be at the margin of the congregation's life, but rather a particular expression of what is implicit throughout all worship and activity within the life of the church. For example, sharing in the Lord's Supper reminds us that Christ is our companion and guest at every meal and meeting. We conduct designated healing services so that we might become aware that every activity of the church is meant to incarnate the reign of God and God's healing dream of shalom. As surprising as it may seem, the capital campaign, budget meeting, social committee, nursery, and youth group can mediate divine healing as effectively as designated healing services, when we recognize that in all its varied tasks, the church is called to only *one* thing —to obey Jesus' command to teach, preach, and heal—in our unique time and place.

chapter two

Healing Homilies

*A*s he walked along, he saw a man blind from birth. His *disciples asked him, "Rabbi, who sinned, this man or his parents, that he was born blind?" Jesus answered, "Neither this man nor his parents sinned; he was born blind so that God's works might be revealed in him. We must work the works of [God] who sent me while it is day; night is coming when no one can work. As long as I am in the world, I am the light of the world." When he had said this, he spat on the ground and made mud with the saliva and spread the mud on the man's eyes, saying to him, "Go, wash in the pool of Siloam" (which means Sent). Then he went and washed and came back able to see.* (John 9:1–7)

As Christians, we affirm that Jesus the healer was God's word made flesh. He not only declared God's reign of healing and shalom, he also embodied God's healing word through companionship with sinners and solidarity with the sick and unclean. The healer from Nazareth revealed God's love by his words, touch, and welcoming spirit.

The healing ministry of the church can find guidance and inspiration in the gospel healing narratives that seamlessly join word and deed. Virtually every healing story has an empowering theological nugget embedded within it that invites us to reflect on God's presence in our own healing journeys. While most readers focus on the specific diseases (leprosy, palsy, blindness, etc.) or the methodologies of healing (touch, exorcism, forgiveness, application of folk remedies, or distant power), the discerning reader will notice that many stories also present a brief theological commentary on the nature of God, the extent of God's care for the lost, the social and theological reality of illness, and the role of humankind in the healing process. Take a moment to reflect on your favorite gospel healing narratives. What theological insights do you find in them? In the story of the healing of the man blind from birth, Jesus confronts, albeit elliptically, the popular theological affirmation that persons always get what they deserve in terms of health and illness. According to popular theology then and now, sin eventuates in poverty and ill health, while righteousness leads to physical well-being and financial success.

In contrast to the popular theology of the time, Jesus asserts that responding to human need is a better test of a person's relationship to God than repeating apparently orthodox theological doctrines (John 9:1–7). The healing of the woman with the flow of blood points to the connection between faith and physical and spiritual transformation, but also portrays the necessity of a divine-human partnership in the healing process (Luke 8:43–48). In response to the plea of a leper, Jesus proclaims, "I do choose" to make him clean, and heals by his touch both the social stigma and the disease that had destroyed the leper's life (Luke 5:12–13).

Jesus expands God's circle of love beyond the boundaries of Israel in healing the centurion's servant, but also affirms that God responds to the prayers of the faithful, even if they come from other religious and ethnic communities (Luke 7:1–10). To the man let down through the roof by his friends, Jesus asserts that the faith of others can be just as significant as one's own faith in healing the sick and that there may be, in certain cases, a connection between the experience of forgiveness and physical well-being (Luke 5:18–26). Jesus reflected on the nature of the Sabbath as a sacred time for healing and comfort as well as study and worship in the theological prelude to the healing of a man with a withered hand (Luke 6: 6–11).

Whole-person understandings of worship and witness join healing words with healing acts to transform persons and communities. Preaching finds its home in the community at worship. Jesus' first public teaching (Luke 4:18–19) and his great commission to his followers linked preaching the good news of God's reign with acts of power that healed the sick, defeated the demonic, and embraced the outcast (Mark 16:17–18). Today, these same healing forces may be released at any worship service or caring encounter. In the context of worship, preaching focuses our hearts and minds on God's aim at justice, peace, and wholeness.

HEALING PREACHING

Nearly two decades ago at a preaching workshop at Kirkridge Retreat and Conference Center, noted preacher and homiletics professor Ernie Campbell proclaimed that there are really only two kinds of persons in the world—those who are in God's hands and know it, and those who are in God's hands and don't know it. Campbell asserted that gospel preaching announces that, in life and death, we are always in God's hands. Campbell's affirmation illuminates the task of preaching the healing narratives of scripture. Good preaching is grounded in good theology and revealed in good practice. Healing preaching is grounded in a lively dialogue with God's desire for wholeness, or shalom, in scripture; the community faith; the preacher's own experience of health, illness, and spiritual transformation; and the divine presence in the human and non-human world. In the spirit of Campbell, we can affirm that there are only two kinds of persons in the world—those who are aware of God's healing touch in their lives, and those who are not! Our lack of awareness may temporarily block God's will in our lives, but it never ultimately thwarts God's holy desire for healing and wholeness for ourselves and those we love. We are all in need of healing, although most of the time we are unaware of this deep need. Healing homilies awaken our need for wholeness in light of God's desire that all persons might have abundant life.

Preaching is profoundly relational in nature. Sadly, some preaching alienates persons from God's healing touch, on the one hand, by blaming the victim, singling out persons with disabilities, condemning persons for their sexual orientation, or claiming that illness is God's will; and, on the other hand, by portraying God as disinterested or impotent in responding to our needs. As the experiences of persons of color, women, gays and lesbians, and persons with disabilities testify, our theological language can heal or hurt. Our inner self-talk can demean and diminish not only ourselves but other persons. Our words and thoughts, spoken and unspoken, can also limit our vision of what God can do in our lives and congregations.

When Jesus told the man with leprosy "I do choose" to heal you, he opened a world of healing possibilities where previously there had been hopeless resignation. In challenging the crowd's belief that Jairus' daughter was dead and dismissing the naysayers from her room, Jesus created a healing circle that enabled God's power to awaken her to a new life (Mark 5:22–24, 35–43). In commanding a man who had been paralyzed nearly forty years to stand up, Jesus created the spiritual conditions that enabled him to take up his bed and walk.

Healing preaching is grounded in healthy and life-supporting theology and worship. In the first chapter, we charted the outlines of a theological foundation for healing worship. In this chapter, we will explore in greater depth how the interplay of theology and spiritual formation can enable preaching to be a more effective medium of healing and wholeness for the preacher and her or his congregation.

Theology is an intricately woven constellation of affirmations, grounded in the dynamic interplay of the biblical tradition, the history of the church, the wisdom of spiritual guides, cultural and scientific insight, and our own experience of God's touch. In the spirit of the Hebraic understanding of God's word (*dabhar*) as the medium of divine creation in the world and in human history, our healing words can be factors in the transformation of minds, bodies, spirits, and relationships. Healing theology renews our minds and liberates transformative physical, emotional, and relational energies in our lives. When such transformative energy is released in the community of faith or an intimate pastoral encounter, lives are changed and miracles occur— new insights emerge, pain is relieved, and diseases are cured.

HEALING AFFIRMATIONS

Our healing words arise from our commitment to embody God's "prophetic imagination" by sharing God's alternative vision of ourselves and the world.[1] Healing theology is grounded in a number of central affirmations that shape the way we experience the world, ourselves, and the divine possibilities in our lives. Healthy theological affirmations promote the healing of our attitudes and beliefs and enable us to see and act in new and creative ways. Theological affirmations shape both the preacher and her or his preaching as they enable us to look at scripture through the lens of a healing hermeneutic.

The affirmations of the church, when interpreted in a manner congruent with God's healing desire for our scientific age, present a radical and life-changing vision of reality. Listen to the following affirmations from the point of view of one of Jesus' healing partners or a person in search of healing in your congregation. Living with affirmations will transform the pastor's spiritual life, preaching, and attitudes toward sickness and healing. They will open the door to God's energy in new and surprising ways. The following theological affirmations build upon the healing theology articulated in chapter one.

God is present as our healing companion in each moment and every life situation. Healthy theology is grounded in lived omnipresence, the practical recognition that all things reflect God's loving care. There are no God-forsaken places if God is the one in whom "we live and move and have our being" (Acts 17:28). The truth of Psalm 139, written from the perspective of the three-story universe, reminds us that we are not lost in unfeeling cosmos, but intimately related to the Divine Companion, whose handiwork is present in the fifteen-billion-year adventure of cosmic evolution.

God is the Living Word who brings forth each moment of experience. In every situation, there is a point of contact that joins God and creation. In each moment, we can affirm that "softly and tenderly Jesus is calling." Healing preaching enables us to experience God as an intimate and ever-present force for wholeness and recovery, regardless of our physical or mental health. Healing preaching enables us to experience God's personal and intimate call in our lives. Even in the darkest night, we can affirm that nothing can separate us from the love of God (Romans 8:38–39).

> Where can I go from your spirit? Or where can I flee from your presence?
>
> If I ascend to heaven, you are there; if I make my bed in Sheol, you are there. If I take the wings of the morning and settle at the farthest limits of the sea, even there your hand shall lead me, and your right hand shall hold me fast.
>
> If I say, "Surely the darkness shall cover me, and the light around me become night," even the darkness is not dark to you; the night is as bright as the day, for darkness is as light to you. (Psalm 139:7–12)

Healing theology proclaims that wherever we are, God is with us, whether receiving chemotherapy treatments, sitting in the doctor's waiting room, or grieving at the graveside. Even if our lives are enveloped in the darkness of depression, God is still our closest companion and comforter. The healing preacher announces the nearness of God as well as God's constant challenge to new life in all of life's events. Healing homilies do not deny trauma, disease, and despair but place them in the larger perspective of God's loving companionship. *The ever-present God is the source of new and creative insights and possibilities for us in every life situation.* The apostle Paul describes God's presence in terms of the Spirit's "sighs too deep for words" (Romans 8:26). Moment by moment, God provides creative alternatives to the present situation. God's presence is the dynamic ground and lively inspiration of each moment of experience. God challenges us to embrace new possibilities and adventures in every challenging situation. The divine restlessness urges us to become God's willing partners in shaping the concrete reality of the reign of God in the here and now. When we pray "your kingdom come, your will be done, on earth as it is in heaven," we are asking for God to enable us to reflect God's plan for the world and our lives in their totality (Matthew 6:10). We are not bound by the past or our current physical condition, but may freely choose to become "a new creation" through God's healing grace. Though our lives are conditioned by many factors beyond our control, God urges us to claim the life-transforming freedom and creativity that is ours. The God whose character is revealed in Jesus' healing ministry is not an indifferent cosmic energy, as some new age thinkers suggest, but a passionate, lively, personal Center of Life whose love joins the cosmic and individual transformation in each moment of experience.

The preacher's challenge is to awaken people to those ubiquitous and universal Spirit-filled "sighs too deep for words" that are our deepest reality. Revelation and healing are universal and dynamic. Preaching enables us to claim God's insight and healing touch in the concreteness of our lives. Preaching reveals God's hidden word and enables us to embrace God's healing presence. Accordingly, the words we choose and the way we express them can enhance or diminish the array of divine healing possibilities available for ourselves and our congregations. When we awaken to God's intimate healing touch, we become God's partners in healing the world one person and situation at a time.

God unambiguously seeks abundant life for us and all creation. Although sin, sickness, and conflict may hide the presence of God in our lives, the deepest reality of our lives and the world is God's desire for abundant life. While God is not the only reality that shapes our lives, God works within the concreteness of our health situation to bring about healing and wholeness. We can face chronic and critical illness with courage and hope, knowing that we are not alone and that God is on our side. This life-affirming optimism enables us to face the stark realities of life and death with awareness that even in the "valley of the shadow of death" God is with us as the source of healing possibilities. As the prologue of John's gospel proclaims, "The light shines in the darkness, and the darkness did not overcome it" (John 1:5). The healing word places our lives in the context of God's constant and enduring love and awakens us to the unique manifestations of God's love in our lives.

THE HEALED AND HEALING PREACHER

Pastoral ministry is profoundly incarnational. Beyond a commitment to learning and growing in the techniques and arts of ministry, church administration, evangelism, and pastoral care, the primary tool of pastoral ministry is the pastor's own spiritual life and commitment to the ongoing process of personal and relational healing. Preparing to preach the healing narratives found in the Gospels, New Testament historical writings and Epistles, and Hebraic scriptures involves integrating study, spiritual formation, and personal healing. Without a commitment to intellectual excellence, based on a critical understanding of scripture, the Christian theological tradition, and the most insightful thinking in psychology, literature, and spirituality and health, our sermons and meditations will be hollow and superficial.

As healing pastors, our vocation is to love God with our minds as well as our hearts even as we seek our own personal healing and transformation. Accordingly, the most successful healing ministries are grounded in the interplay of serious spiritual, biblical, theological, cultural, and medical reflection. Intellectual honesty compels us to ask hard questions about God's presence in our lives and in the healings of Jesus. Healthy theological reflection enables us to separate the wheat from the chaff in today's healing movements, both within and beyond Christianity, as well as to build bridges with Western medicine, complementary health care, and other religious traditions.

Faith is a matter of the heart and body as well as the mind. In reflecting on his own religious struggles, spiritual guide Howard Thurman once noted that while we may know spiritual truths with our minds, our bodies and emotions often need to catch up with the intellect. Preaching the healing narratives of scripture is a whole-person enterprise that challenges the pastor to grow in terms of her or his own spiritual life, relationships, and professional well-being as well as knowledge of scripture and theology.

There are many excellent books on the sermon preparation and delivery.[2] My goal here is to focus on a task that is often neglected in courses on preaching and worship—the ongoing spiritual formation of the preacher. A preacher's spiritual preparation, embodied in the whole of her or his life, but focused week by week on the community's worship, is reflected whenever he or she stands at the pulpit or prays publicly. What is hidden and personal will eventually be revealed in the quality of one's public preaching and pastoral encounters. The preacher's passion for healing and experience of the Holy shines through her whole being in ways that give power and integrity to the preached word. The commitment to the preacher's own intellectual, spiritual, physical, and relational wholeness gives credibility to the preached word.

The following practices, though not exhaustive, enable a pastor to share the good news of divine healing authentically with her or his fullest being. These practices join the preacher's own spiritual transformation with her or his commitment to insightful and life-transforming preaching. They enable the pastor to see her or his life as "*lectio divina*"—a holy revelation of God's desire for healing. In this section, I will focus on how spiritual practices shape the process of preaching and the preaching event by shaping the preacher's own process of spiritual healing. In chapter five, I will provide a wholistic vision of pastoral spirituality that will enable the pastor to claim her or his vocation as a "healed healer."

First, *healing preaching is grounded in a commitment to a life of prayer and contemplation.* In the midst of social and cultural upheaval, the Psalmist counsels, "Be still, and know that I am God!" (Psalm 46:10). Although I believe that the healer of Nazareth was constantly in connection with God's aim at healing and wholeness, Jesus' ministry was enlivened by a commitment to prayer and solitude. After a day of healing, preaching, and teaching, "at daybreak [Jesus] departed and went into a deserted place." But, as many pastors can confirm, the moment Jesus sought a quiet place to pray, "the crowds were looking for him" (Luke 4:42). The phone rings, a parishioner stops by, or we become distracted by our own inner agenda. Still, Jesus' contemplative hours enabled him to address the crowd's interruptions that day and throughout his ministry with grace and honesty.

Prayer and silence are essential to creative, healing ministry and preaching. In moments of intentional silence, we align ourselves with God's presence in our lives. We experience God's will in the ubiquitous and intimate insights and synchronous encounters. In times of prayerful silence, we discover a deeper divine silence that enables us to face the mysteries of life and death with quiet confidence and to sit silently without defensiveness or the need to fill the silence with chatter when we face suffering and death with our parishioners and their families. In times of quiet centering, insights surface that shape the content and form of our sermons.

As I prepare for a sermon, I find that intentional times of silence center me spiritually and allow lively images and helpful insights to flow into my mind. When insights arise, I momentarily file them away in my unconscious mind with the expectation that they will be available when I return to my study.

There are many ancient and contemporary patterns of prayer and meditation that provide insight and passion to our healing sermons. Some pastors commit themselves to sheer silence amid their busy schedules. In silent contemplation, they experience the "inner light of Christ," to use the Quaker image, and see that same light in all its various disguises throughout their pastoral encounters. Each morning or afternoon, they simply follow the Psalmist's counsel to "be still" in the divine presence. Other pastors find God's deep healing through breath prayers. As Psalm 150 proclaims, "Let everything that breathes praise [God]!" While taking one's morning walk or swimming laps, every breath can be a healing breath. Every breath can be an opportunity to breathe in God's healing spirit. Because breathing is a physical necessity, the commitment to prayerful deep breathing centers and heals both our conscious and unconscious mind while it relaxes and grounds our bodies. In John's account of the coming of the Holy Spirit, Jesus promises his peace to his disciples, and then breathes on them as a sign of God's Holy Spirit entering their lives (John 20:19–23). Could it be that we are breathing in synch with the healer of Nazareth and do not know it? What would your day be like if you breathed in God's presence as you left home for the office, answered the phone, prepared for the Sunday service, mediated a church conflict, or made a pastoral call?

Thirty years ago, spiritual teacher Allan Armstrong Hunter taught my wife and me a simple breath prayer that we both still use today: "I breathe the spirit deeply in, and blow it gratefully out again." Many Christians have been inspired by the Vietnamese Buddhist teacher Thich Naht Hanh, who teaches a simple breath prayer: "Breathing in, I calm my body. Breathing out, I smile." Conscious and mindful breathing and smiling, described by Thich Naht Hanh as "mouth yoga," keeps us in touch with our ever-changing emotional life and reminds us that peace is just a breath away.[3] I find that gentle and conscious breathing opens the doors to the higher creativity that is often blocked by perfectionism and anxiety.

Many pastors practice "centering prayer," a simple meditative prayer revived by Thomas Keating and Basil Pennington. In centering prayer, we place our lives in God's presence prayerfully as we focus on a prayer word (such as "peace," "joy," "Christ," "love," "light," "healing"). When we experience mental or external distractions, we simply return to our prayer word without judgment or self-criticism. We conclude fifteen to twenty minutes of centering prayer with a prayer of thanksgiving for God's presence in our lives.

What is good for the spirit has been found to be good for the body. Practitioners of various meditative prayer forms, from centering prayer and transcendental meditation to Zen meditation and Quaker silence, experience what physician Herbert Benson has described as the "relaxation response"— a sense of peace and comfort that is reflected in a reduction in stress and blood pressure along with an enhancement of immune system functioning.[4]

Times of quiet prayer open us to the wellspring of divine creativity. This higher creativity flows into our own minds when we take time simply to listen. Many pastors, such as myself, integrate sermon preparation with walking prayer. In my case, I let the words of scripture flow without any direction as I speed-walk through my neighborhood in Lancaster, Pennsylvania.

Images and thoughts rise to the surface and mental blocks are released. Often my sermon simply writes itself during one of these preaching walks. When I get home, I can hardly wait to turn on my laptop or find a pad of paper and let the Spirit flow through me to the congregation that awaits me Sunday morning. *Healing imagination can transform our lives and our sermons.* In the prophetic tradition, Jesus was an artist of the imagination. His parables awakened people to a new vision of themselves and God's presence in their lives. Revelation comes through the lilies of the field, a seed in the ground, a sparrow in flight, or the adventures of a wayward child. Every moment points beyond itself to the well spring of divine creativity.

Centuries later, Ignatius of Loyola invited his followers to "taste and see" the holy scriptures through imaginative awareness. When we read a biblical narrative, we can imagine the scene or experience ourselves as one of the characters in the story. Take a moment to go back to the beginning of the chapter. Let your mind rest quietly for a moment in the story of a man born blind. Read the words without judgment or analysis. Simply let them flow from the wellspring of divine creativity. Now enter God's story as you imaginatively reflect on this healing encounter.

Imagine that you have been blind from birth. What is it like to be unable to see? How has blindness shaped your life? . . .

Today, you are with your parents, who have cared for you throughout your life. Where are you? What are you doing with them? . . .

You discover that a stranger and his companions have come up beside you. How do you feel when one of the crowd asks, "Who sinned, this man or his parents, that he was born blind?" How do you understand the causes of blindness and other illness? How do you understand the sources of your own blindness? . . .

You listen to Jesus' response. How do you feel when he says that you are not responsible for your blindness? Then, you feel Jesus' touch. You feel him applying mud on your eyes. What does his healing touch feel like? What is your immediate response to Jesus' action? . . .

Jesus tells you to go to the pool and wash your face. Who takes you to the pool? (Or, do you simply go alone?) How do you feel as you walk toward the pool? Experience the coolness of the water as you wash your face and eyes. What happens? Are you able to see? What is the world like as you see it for the first time? How does it feel to be able to see the world? Do things become more visibly clear to you? . . .

You and companions return to Jesus. What does he say to you? What response do you make to him? Now that you can see, what would you really want to see? . . .

As you conclude, make a commitment to keep your senses open to God's presence in your daily life. . . .

Healing imagination opens our senses to scripture in its fullness and gives life to our theological reflections. In prayerfully entering the scripture as a participant, we can gain greater sensitivity to persons with disabilities and those who face chronic and life-threatening illness. We are also enabled without defensiveness to enter more fully into our own experience of health and illness. We may even experience our own inner healing as we imaginatively encounter the healer from Nazareth in our dialogue with scripture.

Through imaginative prayer, we can become any character within the passage, seeing the healing from her or his point of view. Then, as we live imaginatively with the scripture, we are able to invite our congregations to see themselves imaginatively as touching and being touched by God in their encounters with the healer from Nazareth.

Holy reading can open up new dimensions of the healing stories. For centuries, Christians have experienced God's intimate word through the practice of *lectio divina* or holy reading. Taught initially by Benedict of Narsia, this practice helps us discover the image or word that scripture speaks to us today.[5] Grounded in the belief that divine inspiration is present in the reading of scripture, *lectio divina* invites us, first of all, simply to listen for the word of God in the words of scripture. Read the scripture aloud, if possible, hearing its nuances and experiencing its cadence. After a second or third reading, let it "soak" in during a time of silence. You may choose to walk meditatively or simply close your eyes in reflection. In this time of disciplined silence, does a word or image emerge? If you experience this word or image as coming from God, take time to meditate upon it, repeating it or imaging it. Ask yourself, "What does this word or image mean in my life today? What would happen if I acted on this scripture? What word or image might this scripture speak to my congregation today? If we really believed it, how would our congregation be transformed?"

The word or image you receive joins wholistically both hemispheres of the brain and heals the chasm between mind and heart. It enables pastors to claim their own voice in preaching and support their parishioners' creative and life-affirming understandings of scripture. *Lectio divina* also enables the pastor and her or his community to go beyond popular as well as purely rationalistic interpretations of scripture in order to experience God's healing word for today. In holy reading, we wrestle with difficult passages in scripture, not to ease our discomfort with them, but to experience deeper understandings that enable us to experience creatively the challenge of reading scripture today. Further, through the use of *lectio divina*, the pastor can identify the many, often overlooked facets of a familiar scripture. Like prayerful imagination, *lectio divina* allows the healing text to become a lively, credible, and contemporary word to the preacher and the congregation.

I find *lectio divina*, or what my wife Rev. Dr. Kate Epperly describes as "wholly reading," especially helpful when I cannot envisage alternatives to traditional and unimaginative interpretations of scripture passages. In my walking practice of holy reading, I experience unexpected and novel insights into scripture that liberate my imagination in such a way that I discover new and lively understandings that take me beyond traditional and popular interpretations of scriptural passages.

Healing affirmations can transform your preaching and your personal life. Within virtually all the healing stories, you can find a theological affirmation that will promote healing and wholeness in your life and in the life of the congregation. Spiritual affirmations are short, theological statements that describe the deeper realities of life. When we live with affirmations, repeating them on a regular basis, they contribute to the healing of our negative thinking and open our minds to larger dimensions of reality.

Jesus used affirmations to awaken the experience of divine possibility in the lives of his first followers. Just think of the power hidden in Jesus' affirmations of his followers:

— You are the light of the world.

— You are the salt of the earth.

— You can do greater things than I have done.

— Your faith has made you well.

The apostle Paul's writings are also a wellspring of affirmations that empower and transform persons who use them as a lens through which to see themselves and God's presence in the world.

— My God shall supply all my needs.

— Nothing can separate me from the love of God.

— My body is the temple of God.

— I can do all things through Christ who strengthens me.

In preparing a healing sermon or meditation, it is helpful to look for a short statement that describes its deepest meaning for your life. The affirmation can arise out of the practice of *wholly reading* (*lectio divina*) or a simple reading of the scripture narrative. Take a moment to read the scripture found at the beginning of this chapter. What affirmations can you claim in the scripture? Take a deep breath and repeat the affirmation with each breath or step you take. Let the living word enlighten and enliven your mind.[6]

As I read the passage with which this chapter began, I found the following affirmations that can be used as a center point around which to weave a sermon or meditation.

— God is the source of healing, not illness.

— I take my medicine in a holy way.

— I work with Christ to bring healing to my world.

— My work is guided by the light of God.

Preaching is an intimate revelation of the preacher's personal encounter with God's presence in scripture, culture, congregational life, tradition, and personal experience. Healing preaching encompasses the totality of the pastor's life from Sunday to Sunday. It emerges not only from theological reflection and bible study but also imagination, memory, and sensitivity to others' experience. In living with the healing stories of the Bible, the pastor becomes a medium of grace and insight to the congregation as her or his sermons address difficult questions in innovative ways that encompass body, mind, spirit, relationships, and the political realm. Commitment to the spiritual disciplines such as those outlined above also promotes the pastor's own personal and professional well-being and enhances the pastor's sensitivity to persons in pain and ability to mediate God's healing presence to desperate and hopeless persons.

chapter three

Healing Rituals

*T*hen *he returned from the region of Tyre, and went by the
way of Sidon towards the Sea of Galilee, in the region of
Decapolis. They brought to him a deaf man who had an
impediment in his speech; and they begged him to lay his hand
on him. He took him aside in private, away from the crowd,
and put his fingers into his ears, and he spat and touched his
tongue. Then looking up to heaven, he sighed and said to him,
"Ephpatha," that is, "Be opened." And immediately his ears
were opened, his tongue was released, and he spoke plainly.*
(Mark 7:31–35)

*Are any among you suffering? They should pray. Are any
cheerful? They should sing songs of praise. Are any among you
sick? They should call for the elders of the church and have
them pray over them, anointing them with oil in the name of
the Lord. The prayer of faith will save the sick, and the Lord
will raise them up; and anyone who has committed sins will be
forgiven. Therefore confess your sins to one another, and pray
for one another, so that you may be healed. The prayer of the
righteous is powerful and effective.* (James 5:13–16)

Healing is a profoundly social phenomenon. When persons are
sick, they call upon friends for support, make appointments
with their doctors, and cancel meetings and social engagements.

While illness is deeply personal, its impact is never entirely individual. Every illness has social as well as personal meanings. Serious illness disrupts families, congregations, businesses, and communities. Certain illnesses, such as cancer, are identified with death, despite the rising recovery rate. Other illnesses, such as AIDS, are associated with punishment for sin in certain conservative religious communities and with heroism in more progressive communities.

Worship is also a profoundly social phenomenon. Healing worship is the primary antidote to experiences of alienation and powerlessness. Healing services gather persons for mutual support and affirmation, honest confrontation with pain, and wrestling with God, all in the context of the community's affirmation that even in the midst of sickness and death, God is present in our lives and in the healing touch of companions in faith. Worship creates a world in which we may hope for healings and cures by placing our wounds in the hands of God and a healing community. In the spirit of the Psalms, nothing is off limits in healing worship. We come as we are, with the awareness that God's extravagant welcome accepts us just as we are. Pastor Frey's healing service, described in chapter one, regularly brings together a small group of persons for intercession, scripture, song, and touch. Over the years, this small group has become a community of healing companions who support each other through prayer, phone calls, and rides to medical appointments. Her congregation's well-attended Sunday service also gathers people from throughout the community for worship, study, and social conversation. The community breaks bread at the altar and also in the social hall during the coffee hour. Within and beyond the worship service, supportive and healing friendships that extend over decades are forged. Grounded in their faith in God and commitment to their religious community, those who were once strangers become intimates as they comfort one another in pain and celebrate with each other in success.

Within the body of Christ, we affirm the profound interdependence of life. We recognize that we contribute to each other's well-being and require each other's prayerful support if we are to flourish in body, mind, and spirit. We discover our own personal gifts and vocations as we participate in a community that both supports and challenges us. In authentic worship, our spirits are enlarged as we discover that the well-being of others contributes to our own well-being, and our own well-being is endangered if others are left behind. As the apostle Paul proclaims:

> For just as the body is one and has many members, and all the members of the body, though many, are one body, so it is with Christ. For in the one Spirit we were all baptized into one body —Jews or Greeks, slaves or free—and we were all made to drink of one Spirit. . . . If one member suffers, all suffer together with it; if one member is honored, all rejoice together with it.
> Now you are the body of Christ and individually members of it. (1 Corinthians 12:12–13, 26–27)

Healing worship connects us with God, one another, and our own deepest selves. This prayerful connectedness releases a power that transforms mind, body, spirit, relationships, and social structures. Through our prayers, scriptures, hymns, and spiritual reflections, the community of faith aligns itself with God's deeper, but often unrecognized, healing desire for the congregation, its individual members, and the communities that encompass it. The rituals we live by—prayer, communion, healing touch, anointing, and scripture—shape our identities, transform our lives, and create a world in which unexpected possibilities burst forth. Even without the preached word, the ritual acts of touch, prayer, and anointing create a spiritual field of force that opens us to God's ever-present and graceful healing touch.

The early Christian communities, no doubt, also practiced their faith in a variety of liturgical forms as they embraced and transformed Jewish rituals in the context of the Greco-Roman world. While there is no clear evidence of liturgies solely dedicated to personal and corporate healing within the New Testament, it is obvious that the early church saw the healing of mind, body, and spirit as essential to proclaiming the gospel of Jesus Christ. Inspired by the presence of the Holy Spirit, the earliest Christians expected signs and wonders in the context of worship, pastoral care, and interpersonal relationships:

> Now many signs and wonders were done among the people through the Apostles. And they were together in Solomon's Portico. . . . A great number of people would also gather from the towns around Jerusalem, bringing the sick and those tormented by unclean spirits, and they all were cured. (Acts 5:12, 16)

Through hospitality, worship, prayer, healing, and preaching, the early church responded to the deepest spiritual and physical needs of first century persons. Today, the church has a similar vocation. In light of growing interest in spiritual formation, personal well-being, complementary medicine, and the role of spiritual practices in promoting health and healing, mainstream and progressive congregations are called to be places of spiritual and physical healing for persons in search of wholeness of mind, body, and spirit. I believe the creative and open-spirited integration of spiritual formation and healing of mind, body, spirit, and emotions may be mainstream and progressive Christianity's greatest evangelistic tool in the twenty-first century.

MODELS OF HEALING

While there are no explicit models of individual or corporate healing services in the New Testament, our scriptural guides in reflecting on today's healing services will be Luke's account of Jesus' encounter with a man with hearing and speech impairment and the Letter of James' liturgical counsel to a consortium of first century congregations. In creating healing liturgies for our time, the church's primary task is to integrate the wisdom of scripture with evolving understandings of God, spiritual formation, complementary and Western medicine, and the healing process. Although a living faith is not bound to the structures or the words of earlier Christians, nevertheless, spiritual maturity calls us to acknowledge and integrate the insights of earlier healing liturgies and narratives as we respond to the unique challenges and possibilities of our time.

Jesus' response to the man with hearing and speech impediments joins both word and touch (Mark 7:31–35). Called upon to mediate God's healing touch through the laying on of hands, Jesus takes this unnamed man aside for an intimate healing moment. In so doing, Jesus' actions remind us that healing services may be individual as well as corporate in nature.

In this intimate healing encounter, Jesus touches the man's ears and tongue and then turns his own attention toward the source of healing energy by gazing symbolically at the heavens. We can imagine Jesus turning toward the heavens in order to align his spirit with the divine spirit. I believe that in this moment of quiet centering, Jesus "sighs" as a means of focusing on the Divine Life, manifest in the healing and creative breath of God that permeates all things. In the interplay of inhaling and exhaling, Jesus expands his own healing "center" to embrace spiritually and physically the one who stands before him in the circle of God's universal love and energy. Perhaps, Jesus' healing ritual enabled the man to turn his attention from his life-constricting ailments to God's vast and creative healing presence and, thus, become a partner with God and the healer Jesus in his own healing process.

To the man whose disabilities had distanced him from others throughout his life, Jesus gives a healing word—"be opened"— as he touches him. Clearly, word, touch, theology, and ritual, are joined as a means of focusing and opening him to God's ever-present healing energy. In the divine-human partnership embodied in Jesus' healing ministry, this man's willingness to be touched breaks down the barriers that had once separated him from others and allows God's desire for wholeness to transform his life.

Within this intimate encounter, we find a simple, yet powerful, model for worship that integrates word, touch, and silence. As we look at this healing encounter, we can see a gentle yet life-transforming liturgical pattern:

1. Greeting and welcome (creating an intimate healing environment);

2. Healing touch, joined with the most basic physical medium (spittle) in order to create a point of focus for divine healing and human openness;

3. Prayer and spiritual centering joining the healer and his companion and opening both to a wider experience of God's loving energy (the healing breath);

4. Healing words that further open the healer and his companion to God's healing touch (healing affirmation or command);

5. Response to the healing encounter (the man's recognition of healing).

I believe that this healing encounter is an appropriate model not only for healing prayer with individuals but also for formal services of laying on of hands and anointing. The interplay of touch, focus and centering, and verbal affirmation creates a "healing center" that mediates God's healing desire to human need.

Authentic faith joins words and actions, with theological reflection and interpersonal concern, according to the author of the Epistle of James. Written as a pastoral epistle to Christian communities dispersed throughout the Mediterranean world, the Epistle of James presents a wholistic vision of the Christian faith. According to the author, we cannot just preach about healing, we must initiate healing communities through the interplay of personal integrity and concern for vulnerable persons within the community of faith (James 5:13–16). Our theology and our ritual actions mutually transform and enliven one another in expanding circles of influence.

While the Epistle of James is often seen as a theological response to those who emphasized grace at the expense of social responsibility and personal ethics, James' description of the church as a community of care echoes Paul's affirmation of the body of Christ as an interdependent community of vocation and support. Following the Hebraic vision of shalom, James asserts that the character of individuals and communities is symbiotically related.

A healthy community is made up of persons who affirm one another by word and deed, perform acts of kindness toward persons in need, and practice just economic relationships in the workplace. The spiritual values and compassionate actions of a healthy community create the conditions that nurture the personal virtues of generosity, integrity, and justice. Accordingly, a Christian community is, by definition, a healing environment in which persons share their joys and sorrows with the expectation that the community will respond in prayer, personal support, and healing touch.

While sickness often constricts our vision of reality and limits our relationships, the Letter of James affirms that the reality of sickness calls us to companionship and caring within a healthy Christian community. If anyone is sick, we are told that she should call on the spiritual leaders of the church, who will respond through prayer and laying on of hands either in private or in the context of the community's worship (James 5:13–16). In healing relationships, we discover divine comfort and inspiration in life's most difficult moments. Although the Epistle of James does not present a formal liturgy of healing and wholeness, the epistle describes a simple order of worship that is foundational for both individual and communal healing services:

1. Greeting and welcome of those who are ill by the spiritual leaders (a time of opening and focusing);

2. Prayers of petition and intercession by the spiritual leaders (placing our lives in the broader context of divine healing);

3. Confession of sins and words of forgiveness (breaking down the barriers to healing and accepting the healing power of God's grace);

4. Anointing with oil (mediating God's touch through the use of healing balm);

5. Recognition of healing and personal transformation (opening and accepting the divine power that transforms our lives).

The healing circle described in the Epistle of James integrates spirituality, psychology, theology, and healing touch within a caring and trustworthy environment. Anointing not only symbolizes God's touch but also mediates the medicine of immortality and healing that nurtures body, mind, and spirit. Anointing and laying on of hands remind us that every touch is a healing touch, when it is devoted to actualizing God's reign in the world. Liturgical laying on of hands and anointing with oil also invite us to explore God's healing touch through massage, reiki, and other forms of energy work.[1]

In the intricate interplay of mind, body, spirit, and relationships, the Epistle of James also notes the significance of confession and forgiveness in the healing process. While not identifying sickness and sin in a linear fashion, James recognizes that feelings of alienation and guilt disconnect us from the healing power of God and the healing embrace of our communities of faith (James 5:15–16).

Recently, medical researchers have described the negative impact of guilt and grief on the immune system and overall well-being. Some have suggested the role of the "forgiveness factor" in restoring spiritual, emotional, relational, and physical well-being. In the intricate relationship of body, mind, and spirit, our emotions and attitudes are subtly reflected in bodily well-being.[2] Over time, our emotional life and attitudes can be a significant factor in health and illness. Accordingly, spiritual transformation through forgiveness, the healing of memories, or relational reconciliation may contribute to overall physical well-being.[3]

The Epistle of James notes not only that the "prayer of faith" will save the sick, but also that "the prayer of the righteous is powerful and effective" (James 5:16). We can rejoice that James is intentionally vague in describing the exact characteristics of the prayer of faith and the specific beliefs of the righteous ones. His vagueness reminds us that fidelity to God has many diverse expressions—theologically, spiritually, and liturgically—each of which may meditate God's healing energy, depending on the person or the setting. Nevertheless, we can assert that although prayer always makes a difference, the intensity of our faith in God's healing power and our belief that our prayers make a difference both to God and to those for whom we pray creates a healing environment in which surprising and miraculous outcomes may occur.

The Epistle of James also asserts the importance of the spiritual leader's character and morality in the healing process (James 5:16). The quality of our moral and spiritual lives may enhance or hinder our ability to mediate God's energy through liturgy, healing touch, sacrament, and spiritual formation. As church leaders, we are called to be healing partners in every aspect of our lives, not just during times of worship, church leadership, and healing prayer. Healing partnership with God involves an ongoing and consistent commitment to the interplay of personal faith, spiritual practices, professional self-care, personal integrity and fidelity, and social justice. Pastors must always remember that they are also part of the healing circle and that their faith and behavior can mediate or block the flow of God's healing power within their congregations.

HEALING SERVICES

The spiritual power of the early church lives on in today's liturgical healing services. Grounded in the dynamic spirit of the biblical tradition, contemporary healing services seek to respond to the needs of persons today. Affirming both tradition and novelty, today's healing services mediate a healthy and life-affirming theology that recognizes the importance of spiritual healing as well as physical curing in God's overall aim at healing and wholeness. In this section, I will focus on the healing services of two mainstream Protestant denominations—the United Church of Christ and the Presbyterian Church (USA)—as models for contemporary healing services.[4] These services build on the insights of the Christian liturgical tradition and integrate the formal liturgies of the Roman Catholic, Lutheran, and Episcopal traditions with the liturgical spontaneity of the free church tradition. Just as Jesus employed many techniques to channel God's passion for healing to persons in need, we can affirm and use a variety of worship forms—traditional and contemporary—to open ourselves and our faith communities to God's healing energy.

The preamble to the Order for Healing for Congregational Use from the *Book of Worship: United Church of Christ* presents a theological and historical rationale for healing services within mainstream and progressive Christianity, as follows:

> Services of healing have a biblical heritage appropriate for the full life of a local church. Anointing and the laying on of hands are acts closely related to the covenant of faithful love between God and Israel and between God and the church. . . . In the New

Testament, faith, forgiveness of sins, and healing are frequently inseparable but distinct aspects of one experience. . . . Healing, in the Christian sense, is the reintegration of body, mind, emotions, and spirit that permits people, in community, to live life fully in a creation honored by prudent and respectful use.[5]

Avoiding the excesses of many popular faith healers, the United Church of Christ service understands healing as involving synergetic relationships of persons, communities, and political institutions. Although we may always pray for physical relief, authentic healing also includes the experience of spiritual wholeness and God's companionship that may occur even without an obvious physical cure.

God does not promise that we will be spared suffering, but does promise to be with us in our suffering. Trusting that promise, we are enabled to bear the unbearable and recognize God's sustaining nearness in pain, in sickness, and in injury.[6]

Blending ancient and modern language, these denominational services join four themes: divine inspiration in scripture and tradition, growth in faith and spiritual maturity, forgiveness of sin, and human touch. Wholistic in its integration of body and mind and individual and community, the preamble to the United Church of Christ healing service asserts that "private counsel and prayer allow for a deeper exploration of the problems and the resources available for healing, including medical, emotional, and spiritual aid."[7]

In a growing number of congregations, healing is understood as going far beyond the liturgical laying on of hands to embrace congregational health ministries, health care advocacy, architectural accessibility, pastoral care and spiritual formation, and partnership with health care professionals. Health ministry programs recognize that wholistic healing includes not only healing prayers but also pharmaceutical prescriptions and preventative self-care. In the following pages, we will take a deeper look at services from the United Church of Christ and Presbyterian Church (USA), noting how these services contribute to a healing theology and practice within the church. While the focus will be congregational healing worship, the insights of these services are equally applicable for individual healing prayer.

Affirming our faith. Contemporary services of healing begin with the invoking of affirmations of faith in God's healing presence in our lives. Theological affirmations remind us that God's holy desire for us is always healing and wholeness. Within the greeting and opening sentences of the United Church of Christ service, worshippers affirm:

— Whatever you ask in prayer, believe that you will receive it, and you will.

— Jesus said: Heal the sick and tell them, "God's heavenly reign is near you."[8]

The Presbyterian Service for Wholeness with a Congregation notes the interplay of God's passion for healing and our role in the healing process with scriptural affirmations that echo the faith of the early church:[9]

— Those who wait for the Lord shall renew their strength, they shall mount up with wings like eagles, they shall run and not be weary, they shall walk and not faint. (Isaiah 40:31)

— Give praise to God the Almighty, by whose great mercy we have been born anew to a living hope through the resurrection of Jesus Christ from the dead. (1 Peter 1:3)

While these affirmations are grounded in the biblical tradition, they require careful theological reflection and interpretation, since our words shape our self-understanding, interpretation of health and illness, and openness to divine possibility. Sadly, many biblical affirmations can be interpreted in ways that harm rather than heal. The insightful pastor cannot assume that parishioners will understand the theological nuances within each liturgical affirmation. For a person struggling with a terminal illness, what does it mean to say, "Whatever you ask in prayer, believe that you will receive it, and you will?" It is pastorally important, therefore, for healing ministry leaders to assert that while we are called to expect great things from God's presence in our lives, fidelity to God and commitment to spiritual wholeness do not always insure a physical cure. When, despite our prayers and positive thinking, a cure does *not* come, we may unfortunately interpret certain biblical affirmations in ways that suggest that our illness is due to some personal sin, lack of faith, or the working out of God's inscrutable will. While our faith may be the "tipping point" that opens the door to greater manifestations of healing energy in our lives, our faith is only *one* factor in the interplay of disease and healing.

Even the invocation of "Almighty" in our prayers may be challenging to some persons facing serious illness and disability, since the word "almighty" may invoke traditional understandings of the doctrine of divine omnipotence that assert that God unilaterally determines each and every event in our lives. By contrast, a more dynamic vision of God's power in the world assumes that God neither causes all things, including cancer and terrorist attacks, nor knowingly allows them to occur in order to achieve a greater good. In assuming that God is responsible for all events in our lives, we implicitly suggest that God is ambivalent when it comes to responding to our deepest needs. The traditional understanding of divine omnipotence suggests that even though God loves us, our deepest physical and emotional needs are either unimportant to God or are merely means to a greater end that only God can discern. Divine ambivalence is not a healing force! As we seek to understand the nature of divine power and healing, we must ask, "Can God affirm both healing and sickness at the same time?" In contrast to traditional and popular images of divine omnipotence, I believe that recognition of the painful realities of AIDS, cancer, or disability call us to explore creative theological interpretations that define God's power in terms of relationship and love rather than coercion or unilateral activity. Accordingly, I substitute the word "All-loving" or "Holy One" for "Almighty" in healing liturgies as a way of affirming that God's power is always *unambiguously* aimed at healing and abundant life for all.

Within the concreteness of our lives, the extent of God's power may not always be obvious. But, within all things, God is working for good, even those things that God has not chosen but must endure with us as our Healing Companion. Although the All-loving God desires that all creatures experience abundant life and shalom, God's healing desire may take a circuitous route or be thwarted, as it works within the interplay of creaturely freedom and accident. Amid the often mysterious interplay of divine grace and human freedom, the preacher's theological task is to enable persons to trust that God is unambiguously on their side and is working toward wholeness and healing in this life and the next.

Healing scriptures. Today's healing services are grounded in the ministry of Jesus and his command that his followers preach, teach, and heal. Accordingly, scriptures must be chosen with care. While many scripture selections are available for the creative and insightful pastor, the most powerful scriptures are those that emphasize Jesus' healing ministry and God's loving care for persons in all the seasons of life. In their use of scripture, preachers need to affirm clearly that prayer does not always insure a physical cure or a dramatic manifestation of God's power. Manifestations of God's healing desire occur in worship and in private prayer, and bodies and minds can be transformed in the immediacy of the moment. But many, if not most, spiritual healings and physical cures take place quietly and imperceptibly in the gentle and natural processes of growth and renewal of body, mind, and spirit. Like the mustard seed,

God's reign works gently and constantly in our lives and may not fully be discerned for months or years.

It is helpful for persons facing chronic and life-threatening illness to remember that the greatest healing arises from a trusting relationship to a faithful God. While we can always hope and pray for a cure, our ultimate hope is to become partners in God's holy desire for shalom and wholeness.

Healing Words. Healing services join word and touch. Although the focus of a healing service is not the sermon or homily, the task of the preacher is solely to speak a healing word. She is called to present a vision of realistic hope and trust in a God who is unreservedly on our side. While the sermon is always a teaching opportunity, in the context of a healing service the most helpful sermons present an affirmation of faith through a parable, image, or brief word of grace. The preacher's task within the short span and critical moments of the healing service is to nurture faith rather than raise complex theological issues. Accordingly, healing worship must be part of an ongoing congregational emphasis on theological education and pastoral care that explicitly addresses the questions, controversies, and doubts persons have about God's presence in their lives as well as the constructive expression of healing images of God.

Confession and transformation. Our quest for healing is intimately connected with the totality of our lives. Our own personal brokenness and pain cannot be isolated from the realities of sin and injustice in our world. The interconnectedness of life challenges us to seek healing in the affairs of nations and corporations as well as families and individuals. As Gary Gunderson points out, the primary indicator of a child's health in her or his lifetime is the parents' education and economic standing.[10] Physician Kenneth Pelletier suggests that sweat shops, stressful jobs, sexual harassment, job insecurity, gender and race-based limitations can all be hazardous not only to the healthy people directly experiencing them but also to the people around them.[11] The larger circles of planetary health and illness, reflected in the quality of air and water, the intensity of ultraviolet rays, and fair trade and the distribution of food can be a matter of life and death for millions, despite our efforts at prevention. We are intricately bound to one another within the body of Christ in ways which encompass the planet and our nation as well as our congregations. Accordingly, authentic prayers of confession address the impact of our actions on ourselves, others, creation, and ultimately the divine itself. A sensitive pastor, therefore, cannot suggest, even in prayers of confession, a linear one-to-one relationship between individual health and moral behavior, nor blame the victim or sick person or imply that one is responsible for the harmful behavior of others, especially as it relates to physical, emotional, or sexual abuse.

In our emphasis on faith and personal responsibility in the healing process, we must also take into account the influence of the wider community and planet. Healing confession calls us to frame ourselves and our actions within the complexities of an interdependent world. In some cases, confession may free us from unhealthy and inappropriate guilt and responsibility, and open us to our own giftedness and power to transform the world. In other cases, confession may call us to become more assertive and active in our quest for wholeness and self-actualization on a community or planetary level. In the dynamic process of confession and transformation, others may need to let go of personally unhealthy behaviors and withdraw from participation in unjust social systems. Ultimately healthy confession leads us to own the power and freedom, as well as the limitations, of living in a multi-factorial universe.

The process of healthy confession may transform our images of God. We must recognize that we cannot confess our sin and alienation to a deity whose vindictiveness will hold our confession against us. Rather, the One to whom all hearts are open and all desires known uses our self-awareness as a means of empowering, forgiving, and transforming us and others. The

All-loving God "hears us into speech," as Nelle Morton asserts, and calls us to new life in moments of confession.[12] Our expanded awareness of responsibility and grace leads us to actions that support God's healing desire for ourselves and the world.

Healing worship begins with the affirmation that we are created in the image of God. The healing ministry of Jesus suggests that although the reality of sin is tragic and often overwhelming, sin is derivative and never "original" in God's creation or any human life. Confession breaks down the obstacles to God's loving energy and, in the spirit of Jesus' imagery of the vine and branches, reconnects us to the lively and loving vine from which all blessings flow (John 15:1–11).

In this spirit, the Presbyterian worship book utilizes a traditional prayer of confession as a means of opening "to God's healing presence" and "forsaking all that separates us from God and neighbor":

Merciful God, we confess that we have sinned against you in thought, word,and deed, by what we have done, and by what we have left undone. We have not loved you with our whole heart and mind and strength; we have not loved our neighbors as ourselves.[13]

Corporate prayers of confession do not leave us bereft of hope. Confession awakens us as members of faithful communities to divine forgiveness and calls us and others to acts of mercy and transformation. Corporate prayers of confession are fertile ground for the divine-human synergy within which healing, change, and transformation may always be found.

In your mercy, forgive what we have been, help us amend what we are, and direct what we shall be, so that we may delight in your will and walk in your ways, to the glory of your holy name.[14]

The United Church of Christ service of healing affirms the corporate nature of sickness and healing:

> To bear one another's burdens in prayer is a holy privilege. It also demands a willingness to be a channel for God's power. . . . Let us name also our connection with humanity's sins: sins of poverty, war, hunger, injustice, neglect, and discrimination.[15]

In prayer, we ask that God cleanse, forgive, and create in us a new heart and healed spirit. Our healing is never individual but the result of our connectedness with a loving God and a nurturing, supportive, and empowering community of faith that holds us accountable for our individual and corporate behavior.

The declaration of forgiveness or assurance of pardon expresses God's never-ending, always-resourceful love for humankind and all creation. The affirmation of God's acceptance and love sets us free to embrace the healing energy of God without reservation. "I announce with joy that we are forgiven," proclaims the healing pastor. "Anyone who is in Christ is a new creation. The old life has gone; a new life has begun," affirms the empowering pastor. "May the God of mercy, who forgives you all your sins, strengthen you in all goodness, and by the power of the Holy Spirit keep you in eternal life," promises the reassuring pastor. Truly, nothing can separate us from the love of God, nor will God ever cease to call us to new adventures in healing ourselves and the world.

Healing Intercessions. Prayer connects us with God and one another. While prayer is not magic or an attempt to manipulate God's healing presence, the community at prayer contributes to new energy and creates a positive field of force that strengthens the faith of those for whom we pray and, in ways we cannot fully understand, supports God's passion for healing and wholeness. The gospels clearly note that the faith of individuals and supportive friends and family played a significant, though not absolute, role in Jesus' healing ministry. Healing prayers align us with God's desire for abundant life. We become God's healing partners in bringing forth healing possibilities for ourselves and others. Although the Presbyterian service of wholeness invites extemporaneous prayers, it also calls the community to pray for "all who are in need of healing . . . for all who are disabled by injury or illness . . . for all who are troubled by confusion or pain . . . for all whose increasing years bring weariness . . . for all about to undergo surgery . . . for all who cannot sleep . . . for all who practice the healing arts."[16] These phrases cover the broad spectrum of human brokenness and invite us to see our own pain and response-ability in light of the tragedies others are facing. In the moment of silence following each phrase, we may choose to image those for whom we pray surrounded in the circle of divine love or healing light.

The United Church of Christ service of healing asks God "in the power of your Holy Spirit to enter and heal your servant . . . [to] comfort him/her with the assurance of your care and goodness; save him/her from temptation and despair; give him/her patience under affliction; and enable her/him to live the remainder of life in peace."[17] In life and death, and in sickness and in health, our healing prayers remind us that God's presence in our lives and in the community of faith will provide what we need to find shalom in this life and the next.

Anointing and laying on of hands. Jesus healed not only by word, but by touch. Although Jesus provided no specific formula or liturgical language as he anointed or touched persons in need, the breadth of Jesus' healing ministry affirms that liturgical anointing and laying on of hands are not exceptions to God's healing touch. Instead, they are powerful and focused expressions of God's holy desire as revealed in moments as intimate as a parent's loving caress of his child, an adult child's comfort of her confused parent, the passionate embrace of lovers, or the healing touch of massage therapists and practitioners of reiki, body psychotherapy, and therapeutic touch. Healing touch mediates the "real presence" of God in such a way that the innate and God-given recuperative powers of mind, body, and spirit are released.

Anointing with oil symbolizes the spiritual medicine that is mediated by touch, pharmaceuticals, complementary health care, and technological medicine. As a prayer form, healing touch supplemented by anointing with oil connects us to God's healing processes that surround us every day. Holy touch reminds us that, despite our pain and illness, we are always connected to soothing healing powers beyond themselves.

The gathered community is invited to pray for each person as he or she enters the circle of healing to receive anointing or laying on of hands. This circle makes clear that healing is never a solitary enterprise but a reflection of God's dynamic presence in our limited and fallible relationships.

This healing circle is most effective liturgically through the use of several healing stations scattered around a large congregation or in the chancel of a smaller congregation. In the circular format, the collective focus of prayer and touch is shared by each of the participants, giving and receiving laying on of hands as each takes time rotating in and out of the center, regardless of whether a particular lay or clergy person is designated to verbalize the healing prayer. Ideally, the designated clergy or lay leader will also be able to receive the laying on of hands and anointing if desired.

In many congregations, the act of anointing may involve touching each person's forehead with healing oil and making the sign of the cross, the symbol of God's victory over sickness, alienation, and death. As the United Church of Christ healing service affirms:

> On your confession of repentance and faith, you are now anointed with oil in the name of Jesus Christ, for the forgiveness of sins, for the strengthening of your faith, and for healing and peace, according to God's grace and wisdom.[18]

The Presbyterian service for wholeness asks for God's blessing on all who come for anointing and healing touch:

> By your Spirit, come upon all who receive the laying on of hands [who are anointed with this oil], that they may receive your healing touch and be made whole, to the glory of Jesus Christ our Redeemer.[19]

In that same spirit, the United Church of Christ prayer for the laying on of hands affirms:

> I/we lay my/our hands upon you in the name of our Sovereign and Savior Jesus Christ, calling on Christ to uphold and fill you with grace, that you may know the healing power of God's love.[20]

Members of the congregation are invited to seek laying on of hands for their own well-being or "as a channel of God's healing power for someone else," believing that our own faith can be a catalyst for the healing of other persons when we allow ourselves to be a focal point of prayerful energy.

The healing power of thanksgiving. Gratitude is the gift and affirmation of healing and wholeness. The German mystic Meister Eckhardt once stated that "if the only prayer you can say in your whole life is 'thank you,' that would suffice."[21] Regardless of our current situation, gratitude reminds us that we are in God's hands. Gratitude liberates us from the suffocating and life-constricting power of illness and connects us with the universal source of beauty and love. When we say thank you, we acknowledge the giftedness of life and love that sickness can never quench. Despite the painful realities of sickness and death, gratitude enables us to say "yes" to life in its totality.

As healing worship concludes, the United Church of Christ service turns our attention from ourselves to God's abundant life and our vocation to respond to the needs of others. We affirm that the healing power present in Jesus' healing ministry is still alive in our time. God's holy desire, reflected in the incarnation of Christ, is present in all healing encounters, but most powerfully in times of personal and communal prayer and touch.

> We give praise and thanks to you, O God!
> In Jesus Christ, you have given us life;
> brought ministry, forgiveness, healing, and peace;
> commanded the disciples to heal the sick;
> and continued the healing ministry among us to this day.
> Keep us mindful of your love and mercy
> that we may be faithful throughout all our days,
> in the name of Jesus Christ. Amen.[22]

Healing songs. It has been said that to sing is to pray twice. Many persons who would not consider themselves theologians regularly affirm a variety of theological faith formulae and proclaim as they sing their favorite hymns. Like the repetition of the Lord's Prayer or Doxology, the hymns we sing join mind and heart, conscious and unconscious. Swaying, clapping, or tapping our feet, our hymns inspire our bodies and embody our spirit. Singing is truly body prayer! As a whole-person experience, the words we sing are just as important as the words we preach or the creeds we affirm. Just as we choose our words carefully, we must also choose our hymns carefully so that they may theologically edify and aesthetically support God's healing presence in worship and touch. Ultimately the greatest reassurance healing hymnody provides is found in the affirmation of God's faithfulness, love, and healing presence in every moment and situation of life and death.

Although certain contemporary hymnals contain a selection of hymns under the specific heading of healing, virtually every hymnal has hymns that describe God's loving faithfulness to persons in need of healing and wholeness. While the following list of hymns is not exhaustive, it contains hymns that affirm God's universal and unambiguous holy desire for healing and wholeness. All of these hymns are theologically appropriate for worship services that heal, comfort, and sustain.

— "Break Thou the Bread of Life," Mary Lathbury, Alexander Groves, and William Sherwin

— "Breathe on me, Breath of God," Edwin Hatch and Robert Jackson

— "Bring Many Names," Brian Wren and Carlton Young

— "Come, Thou Fount of Every Blessing," Robert Robinson

— "Gather Us In," Marty Haugen

— "God of the Sparrow, God of the Whale," Jaroslav Vajda and Carl Schalk

— "Great is Thy Faithfulness," Thomas Chisholm and William Runyan

— "Guide Me, O Thou Great Jehovah," William Williams and John Hughes

— "Healer of Our Ev'ry Ill," Marty Haugen

— "He Touched Me," William Gaither

— "How Firm a Foundation," John Rippon's *Selection of Hymns*

— "How Like a Gentle Spirit," C. Eric Lincoln and Alfred Morton Smith

— "I Thank You Jesus," Kenneth Morris

— "I Was There to Hear Your Borning Cry," John Ylvisaker

— "It is Well with My Soul," Horatio Spafford and Philip Bliss

— "Just as I am," Charlotte Elliot and William Bradbury

— "My Life Flows On," Robert Lowry

— "Now Thank We All Our God," Martin Rinkart and Johann Cruger

— "On Eagle's Wings," Michael Joncas

— "Precious Lord, Take My Hand," Thomas Dorsey

— "Silence, Frenzied, Unclean Spirit," Thomas Troeger and Carol Doran

— "Standing on the Promises," R. Kelso Carter

— "Strong, Gentle Children," Dan Damon

— "There is a Balm in Gilead," African American Spiritual

— "When Aimless Violence Takes Those We Love," Joy Patterson and Alfred Morton Smith

— "You are My Hiding Place," Michael Ledner

When integrated with healing rituals and healing theology, healing songs convey the intimate, loving presence of God and transform body, mind, spirit, and relationships. Long after the service is over and the sermon theme is forgotten, we may remember a word or tune that will comfort, sustain, and empower us in times of trial. We may hum our faith as we do the dishes or drive to work as a spiritual reminder that in life and in death we belong to God.

Think of the hymns that have changed your life. What hymns nurture your spirit and bring healing to your life? When my mother-in-law's husband of nearly fifty years died, she was sustained each morning as she sung the traditional hymn, "Spirit of the Living God Fall Afresh on Me." Whether singing, humming, or chanting, our hymns open a channel through which God's healing energy flows.

Celebrating communion. Many healing services have, as their centerpiece, the celebration of Holy Communion or the Eucharist. This ritual of sharing the bread and the cup unites us with one another and joins us with the One who healed his disciples in life and death. As the "medicine of immortality," communion embodies the faith we affirm and mediates God's presence to those who seek wholeness for themselves and others.

For those congregations that celebrate open communion, the sacrament also extends God's gift of healing and wholeness to all present. The celebration of communion reminds us that our healing is not an individual blessing, but part of God's universal work of shalom. The Christ who reaches out to feed us in bread and wine sustains our whole being every moment of our lives.

The celebration of communion reminds us that although our pain, like that of the crucified Jesus, is real, it is not the whole story of our own lives or the planetary journey. In thankful praise, we reconnect with the divine vine from whom all blessings flow.

In the Celtic tradition, certain geographical locations are identified as "thin places," where God's presence shines forth. For those pursuing the ministry of healing, all places are thin places and every locale contains a ladder of angels that joins heaven and earth. Therefore, communion is one more opportunity to remember that we are always on holy ground—in our families, schools, workplaces, hospitals, and even broken and diseased bodies. The celebration of communion enables us to recognize that the Risen One who broke bread with grieving followers at Emmaus restores our health through his healing touch and sustaining presence in our lives today.

Healing Sundays. Whether or not it has an explicit time for healing prayer or laying on of hands, every Sunday service celebrates God's presence in life and death. In each Sunday's worship, we proclaim that Christ is alive and still raises the dead and heals the sick. In the spirit of the early Christians, each Sunday is a mini-Easter in which we affirm our faith in God's ability to transform sickness, hopelessness, and death into new and abundant life. While not all churches have healing rituals at their Sunday worship services, many congregations provide monthly opportunities for laying on of hands and intercessory prayer during or following each Sunday's service.

At Palisades Community Church where Rev. Dr. Kate Epperly served as pastor for ten years, an explicit time of healing prayer and laying on of hands was offered on the third Sunday of the month as part of the prayers of the people. Those who sought healing for themselves, or as a channel of healing for others, were invited to gather in a healing circle. As "Dr. Kate" prayed for each person around the circle, the remaining members of the circle laid hands on that person as a sign of the corporate nature of healing. Everyone in the congregation was urged to pray for each person as he or she entered the healing circle.

The third Sunday healing circle was not an exception to the church's concern for healing, but an expression of the congregation's commitment to mediate God's healing presence throughout the week through health care advocacy, reiki healing touch, spiritual formation, courses on health and wholeness, blood pressure screenings, and commitment to economic justice in the nation's capital. During the prayers of the faithful each Sunday morning, a generous time of silence allowed participants to name orally or silently persons in need of God's healing touch. Further, "Dr. Kate" regularly prayed for persons in need and provided reiki healing touch and spiritual counsel for persons at the hospital. Her open-spirited ministry created the expectation that healing prayer was an essential part of the church's ministry.

God's aim at healing encompasses the totality of life. When we gather for times of healing worship or prayerful intercession, we recognize God's unambiguous love and care for each person is present every moment of our lives. In prayerful worship, we touch the Healing God and receive God's touch in return.

chapter four

New Visions of Healing Worship

I appeal to you therefore, brothers and sisters, by the mercies of God, to present your bodies as a living sacrifice, holy and acceptable to God, which is your spiritual worship. Do not be conformed to this world, but be transformed by the renewing of your minds, so that that you may discern what is the will of God—what is good and acceptable and perfect. (Romans 12:1–2)

Worship is a communal adventure in healing and wholeness. We gather together to affirm our interdependence with God and one another as members of the body of Christ. Through sacrament, scripture, and song, we affirm the profound inter-connectedness of life—of minds and bodies, individuals and communities, humankind and the planet—as God's good and growing creation. We come seeking transformation in one another's lives through intercession, touch, gratitude, and praise. Worship unites time and space in the healing of persons and communities. In moments of prayer, we experience *kairos* times that awaken us to God's aim at wholeness. In healing touch, we experience sacred space and holy ground in which God's power is unexpectedly released to comfort, soothe, and heal minds, bodies, spirits, and relationships. Through passing the peace, we find safety, support, and strength to face challenges of body, mind, and spirit. In the synergy of divine and human partnership, we experience miracles of liberation, reconciliation, and well-being.

Whether traditional or informal, contemplative or multimedia, worship is profoundly contextual in nature. To truly heal, worship must join tradition and innovation, familiarity and surprise, in ways that address the deepest needs of the worshipping community. This is especially important as congregations seek to respond to persons who have been injured by punitive and hierarchical images of God and harmful theological explanations of healing and sickness. Further, in this postmodern and pluralistic age, lively healing worship embraces the wisdom of global spirituality, complementary health care and Western medicine, and creative theological reflection. In chapter three, I reflected upon God's healing presence in the context of first century and contemporary denominational liturgical forms of healing worship. In this chapter, we will explore alternative healing services that seek to balance tradition and innovation in their support of the healing journeys of life-long church members as well as the many unchurched or formerly churched who come in search of wholeness and healing.

As a healer, Jesus responded to persons in terms of their unique needs of body, mind, and spirit. While a degree of tradition and uniformity is necessary in order to provide psychological reassurance, safety, and security in difficult times, the concreteness of life and the needs of a congregation challenge each congregation to be adventurous in its quest to be a healing presence in its community. Lively healing energies emerge when attentiveness to the One who is the same yesterday, today, and tomorrow is balanced with awareness that Divine Love is always doing a new and intimate thing.

The services that follow provide imaginative resources for congregational healing ministries. In their liturgical simplicity, they join tradition and novelty. Of course, fidelity to the healing God calls us to shape these services in ways that best respond to the needs and experiences of your community of faith.

HEALING IN THE SPIRIT OF TAIZÉ

Throughout history certain places have been recognized as venues where divinity and humanity, time and eternity meet. Though God is both omnipresent and omni-active, certain places radiate God's presence in the midst of ordinary life. In such places, we experience with Jacob "a ladder of angels" joining earth and heaven or imagine, with William Blake, a universe in a grain of sand. Throughout the ages, spiritual pilgrims have encountered God's holiness in places such as Iona, Lourdes, and Jerusalem. Global spiritual seekers have felt God's energy at Sedona, Arizona; Glastonbury, England; Canyon de Chelley, Arizona; and Findhorn, Scotland. While we identify certain places as holy, the doctrine of divine omnipresence reminds us that any place, on any continent, can be a medium of healing revelation.

For many seekers, the Taizé Community in Cluny, France has become a spiritual community where persons come for healing and new life. Founded by Brother Roger Louis Schutz-Marsauche in 1949, the spiritual aim of the Taizé Community is to be "a parable of community" for a divided Christianity. Taizé was founded to be a place of healing and reconciliation among the scattered denominations of Christianity. The community is composed of nearly a hundred Protestant and Catholic brothers who come from approximately thirty different countries on four continents. But, each summer thousands of young as well as older seekers pilgrimage to Taizé for prayer, meditation, community, and spiritual formation. Constantly evolving to meet the needs of contemporary persons, Taizé seeks to embody the interplay of novelty and tradition on the basis of three central themes:

> The theme of *reconciliation* of Christians, i.e. the ecumenical theme; the theme of *evangelization*, aimed at the crowds of young people from all over the world who sometimes know very

little about the mystery of faith; and the theme of *a Christianity that is creative.*[1]

Guided by a vision of reconciliation, and wholeness, Taizé seeks to heal a broken Christianity—"in the end there is only one Church, a Church which we are wounding, a Church whose one, seamless garment we are tearing apart."[2] Profoundly incarnational, the theological vision of Taizé both universalizes and contextualizes traditional Christology by recognizing that the human and divine that were joined without separation and confusion in the life of Jesus the Christ may also be joined in our own lives.

This quest for incarnational spirituality is most evident in the liturgy of Taizé that joins repetitive chanting and silence within the context of the centered pluralism of the body of Christ. The essentials of living Christianity are expressed in the words of repetitive songs that join heart, mind, and community with the One in whom we live, move, and have our being.

Many congregations in the United States and Canada have initiated Taizé services as part of their commitment to new forms of worship and spirituality. I believe that the Taizé style of worship—blending song, silence, and common prayer—is especially suitable to informal services of healing and wholeness. The repetitive changes transform our conscious mind and then flow into the unconscious, bringing healing to memories, acknowledged and forgotten, and wholeness even to the cellular level.

What follows is a brief service of healing in the spirit of Taizé.[3] While innovation is encouraged, the regular repetition of certain songs or chants enables the words to bring an immediate "relaxation response" to the unconscious as well as conscious mind.

A Taizé Service of Healing and Wholeness

A Time of Gathering and Silence

Song   *Jubilate Deo*[4]

Silence

Song   *Ubi caritas Deus ibi est*[5]

Silence

Scripture

Silence

Confession   *Kyrie Eleison*[6]

Silent confession

Words of assurance

> If anyone is in Christ, he is a new creation.
>
> If anyone is in Christ, she is a new creation.
>
> God's healing touch is upon you.
>
> All is new, all is whole, all is forgiven. Amen.

Song   *Lord Hear Our Prayer* [7]

Intercessions

Song   *Veni Sancte Spiritus*[8]

Anointing and laying on of hands

> *(The community lays hands on the person seeking healing for her–or himself or another as the leader anoints her or him with oil, praying extemporaneously or using a prayer such as "We lay hands upon you and anoint you that you might experience God's healing touch. May God heal you and those for whom you pray in body, mind, spirit, and relationships. In the name of the Father, Son, and Holy Spirit, Creator, Redeemer, and Inspirer of us all. Amen." The laying on of hands may be done in a healing circle or in stations where those seeking prayer may come for the laying on of hands and anointing by designated leaders.)*

Prayers for the reconciliation of the church and planetary
healing

Song   *Dona Nobis Pacem*[9]

Closing circle of healing

*(The community joins hands in a circle as an affirmation of
our unity of Christ, the healing presence that joins us, and
our commitment to pray for one another throughout the
week.)*

A CELTIC CIRCLE OF HEALING

Celtic spirituality provides profound resources for healing and
wholeness, especially for spiritual seekers and persons alienated
by the sin-redemption theology of certain churches. With the
growing interest in ecology and creation-oriented spiritualities,
the robust commitment to an embodied faith characteristic of
Celtic spirituality has contributed to the spiritual formation of
many Christians. Wholistic in nature, Celtic spirituality recognizes that life is dangerous as well as beautiful. Stormy seas,
angry chieftains, and evil spirits abound in the spiritual journey.
Yet, each step of the journey may lead us closer to God. Each
place may become a "thin place" and each task, from milking
the cow to lighting the morning fire, can be a holy work.

Unlike the early Celts, we do not expect to encounter angry
chieftains or banshees along our daily journeys. But, still we
recognize that our world today is also wild and dangerous. We
fear terrorist attacks and the diagnosis of a life-threatening disease. Our technology has not protected us from global warm-
ing, Alzheimer's disease, cancer, or sudden corporate or individual catastrophe. We need to experience God as our creative
companion, inspiring guide, and holy protector in every life situation.

A healing service in the spirit of the Celtic Christianity
affirms God's protection and healing presence through ritual

actions, touch, and movement. Although it recognizes the reality of sin and sickness, Celtic spirituality proclaims, in contrast to traditional interpretations of the doctrine of original sin, the essential goodness of life and the ability of humans to become partners in God's healing of the world.

The Celtic *caim*, or "encircling," with which the service begins expresses Celtic spirituality's confidence in God's intimate and loving care. The prayer of encircling proclaims that, wherever we go, we dwell in the circle of God's love. In this body prayer, typically, one rotates slowly in a clockwise fashion with the hand extended and the index finger inscribing the moving circle.[10]

The prayer of St. Patrick, written in response to the murderous threats of a pagan chieftain, remind the congregation that divine omnipresence is a lived reality—God is our protector and guide in every life situation. The "prayer for the hands" consecrates our daily tasks, whether at home or at work. This prayer is an inspiring prelude to the laying on of hands or a blessing for the day ahead.

A CELTIC CIRCLE OF HEALING AND BLESSING

Prelude   *Music in the Celtic tradition*

A time of quiet prayer

The Celtic encircling

> Loving God, whose love is the circle whose center is
> everywhere and whose circumference is nowhere. We
> place our lives in your circle that we might know the
> wonder of your love and the security of your protection.
> Remind us that nothing in life and death separates us
> from your love in Christ Jesus the healer and friend.
> Amen.

Hymn   *"Be Thou My Vision"*

Scripture

Pastoral meditation

The laying on of hands[11]

(Persons gather in a healing circle for this time of prayer and blessing. Persons seeking healing for themselves and others may enter the center of the circle to receive the blessing of the community.)

May the spirit of the living God, present with us now, enter your body, mind, and spirit, and heal you from all that harms you. May God's peace surround, protect, and guide you. In Christ's name. Amen.

or

God to enfold you.
Christ to touch you.
The Spirit to inspire you.
God of adventurous love,
bless my hands this day.
May I touch all things with love
that all things be blessed.
May I give and receive
God's healing touch in all that I do. Amen.

THE PRAYER OF ST. PATRICK

Christ behind and before me,
Christ beneath and above me,
Christ with me and in me,
Christ around and about me,
Christ on my left and my right,
Christ when I rise in the morning,
Christ when I lie down at night,
Christ in each heart that thinks of me,
Christ in each mouth that speaks of me,
Christ in each eye that sees me,
Christ in each ear that hears me.

CELEBRATING GOD'S HEALING LIGHT (IN THE SPIRIT OF JOHN'S GOSPEL)

John's Gospel proclaims that Christ is the light of the world and that God's creative light enlightens all humans (John 1:1–5, 9). Jesus affirms that his disciples are the "light of the world" and challenges them to let their light shine (Matthew 5:14–16). In the world's religious traditions, light is often identified with God's healing presence. The light that creates the universe in the beginning and in each moment of time permeates every cell of our bodies. Though we turn away from God's healing light and thus diminish its impact on our health and well-being, a service celebrating God's healing light affirms that God's light still shines in the darkness and cannot be quenched by any human hurt or pain.

Many Christian healers such as Agnes Sanford employed the imagery of divine light as an aid in their healing ministries.[12] They invite persons in search of healing to envisage God's healing light permeating every cell in their bodies and surrounding them with divine protection. Services of healing light are especially powerful during the Advent and Christmas Seasons.

AWAKENING TO GOD'S HEALING LIGHT

THE LIGHTING OF THE CANDLES

Greeting	John 1:1–5, 9; Matthew 5:14–16
Hymn	*"I am the Light of the World"*
	(Jim Strathdee, inspired by a poem by Howard Thurman)

OPENING TO GOD'S HEALING LIGHT

Leader: Begin by gentle, focused breathing, letting go of any distractions or tension. Relax from head to toe. Then, begin to image a healing light entering and filling your body. This light, the light of Christ, fills your whole being, bringing healing to mind, body, and spirit. Let the light encompass and transform any places of disease and pain. Conclude by imaging God's healing and protecting light surrounding you.

PRAYERS OF INTERCESSION

Leader: As names of persons or situations are mentioned, imaginatively surround each person in God's healing light. Imagine each one as healthy and whole.

LAYING ON OF HANDS

(Persons may gather in a healing circle or in stations throughout the place of worship.)

Leader: As I lay hands upon you, may God's healing light flow through you to bring wholeness to you and those for whom you pray. The light of Christ transforms and protects you and those for whom you pray. Amen.

Hymn   *"This Little Light of Mine"*

WALKING IN THE LIGHT

Leader: Take a moment, once more, to breathe in God's healing light. Let it flow through your entire being and out your hands and feet. See that light surrounding, connecting, and healing a loved one . . . your church . . . your community . . . the nation . . . the planet . . . Imagine the whole world surrounded and permeated by God's healing light. In your imagination, see the world—from this room to the unknown reaches of the universe—encompassed in God's light.

Closing Hymn   *"We are Marching in the Light of God"*
                       (South African hymn—Siyahamba)

HEALING USING IMAGINATIVE PRAYER

The quest for healing affirms the power of the imagination to transform our lives. In the spirit of the biblical prophets and the healer Jesus, our prayers present and activate alternative visions of reality and provide a way to embody what seems impossible to those whose imaginations are imprisoned by the present moment. Imagination was at the heart of Jesus' ministry of teaching and healing. Jesus' parables shocked and transformed persons' visions of God and their role in God's reign on earth. Jesus saw wisdom givers and leaders in marginalized women and courageous preachers in timid fishermen. He saw children of God in despised tax collectors and equanimity in those possessed by the demonic. Jesus saw the totality of life in terms of God's aim at shalom. Jesus' healing imagination tipped the balance from death to life for Jairus' daughter and for the man at the pool. Jesus even allowed his own imagination to be stretched by the words and actions of others. The challenging response of the Syrophoenician woman inspired Jesus to expand the boundaries of his own understanding of healing to embrace the foreigner and enemy (Mark 7:24–30).

In the Christian tradition, the *Spiritual Exercises* of Ignatius of Loyola focuses on sensate and imaginative interpretations of scripture.[13] When we read a passage, we can envisage ourselves as one of the characters. We can imagine the environment and our companions in the gospel narrative. We can experience ourselves touched by the healer or challenged to expand our understanding of the Sabbath, the words of Jesus, or his hospitality toward the unclean and ostracized. Imagination enables us to become contemporaries with the healer Jesus even as we ground ourselves in our own time and place.

Healing visualizations or imaginative prayers can occur in the context of any healing service or bible study. The key to healing visualizations is, first, to let go of our previous understandings of scripture and the limits we place on God's activity in the world and, second, to respond to the imaginative prayers in our own personal way, which may or may not "go" where the visualization is "designed" to take you. This is especially true for persons who initially have difficulties with guided visualizations. They need to be reminded that they can follow the guided healing visualizations wherever they lead, even if they take a different direction than the leader's suggestions. Simply listening to the words can transform your mind and change your health condition.

When my son was young, I often read to him from the "Choose Your Own Adventure" book series. At each fork in the road, the participant's choice might lead to discovering hidden treasure or to a dungeon. Both choices represented continuing adventures with more choices to come. The same applies to healing visualizations. There is no predetermined goal to our imaginative journeys. But, the imaginative journey is always a spiritual adventure with God as our companion.

While there are many possibilities for using healing visualization in worship, the following service integrates silence and relaxation with personal, imaginative creativity. The liturgy recognizes that many of us need to be still for awhile before we engage in the challenging path of imaginative prayer or *lectio divina*.

A SERVICE OF IMAGINATIVE PRAYER

Greeting   Psalm 150 ("Let everything that breathes praise [God]!")

PRAYER OF AWARENESS

O Healing God, as near to us as each breath, help us to rest in your love. Help us to pause awhile and trust your care. Let your healing light flow in and through us with every breath that we might bless one another and all we meet. In the name of Jesus the healer. Amen.

BREATH PRAYER

In the quiet, let us affirm the Psalmist's words, let everything that breathes praise God. Let us rest in God's presence with each breath. Let each breath be a healing breath. Let

each breath connect us with our healing companions in the
chapel and across the planet.

PRAYER OF CONFESSION

Holy God, you have given us the vision of shalom and
wholeness. You have called us to envisage new and creative
possibilities for our lives. Yet, too often we are imprisoned
by the present moment and our own limited understanding
of your loving care. Awaken our visions that we might
dream of holy impossibilities and embody them by your
grace. In Christ's name. Amen.

WORDS OF ASSURANCE

In Christ, we are a new creation.

We open our hearts, minds, and hands to your unfettered
vision of what we may be as persons and as a community as
companions in your holy adventure.

IMAGINATIVE PRAYER[14]

Reading the scripture

Mark 5:25–34 (the woman with the flow of blood)

Quiet reflection on the scripture

Healing imagination

Take a few moments to imagine a day in the life of the
woman with the flow of blood. For years you have been
struggling with a chronic illness—an illness of mind, body, or
spirit. What illness have you been facing? You have sought
the most advanced treatments but still struggle for well-
being. Your illness has shaped your relationships and professional life. It has also alienated you from other persons.

You hear that the healer Jesus will be in your town. What are
your feelings? Do you want to see him? (At this point, you
may choose simply to stay home. If you decide to stay home,
how do you envisage your future?) . . .

You decide to seek out the healer Jesus. As you walk toward the town center, what does your town look like? Do you see anyone familiar on your way to the heart of town? When you get to the center of town, you find that a crowd is awaiting the healer. What is it like to push your way through the crowd? . . .

Finally, you see Jesus in the distance. What does he look like? How do you feel when you see him? As you push your way toward the healer, you begin to repeat to yourself—"if I only touch him, I will be well . . . if I only touch him, I will be well . . . if I only touch him, I will be well." . . .

You reach out and touch him, and a powerful energy flows from the healer to you. What does it feel like? You sense that something has changed and that you have been healed. . . .

In the midst of the crowd, the healer asks, "Who touched me?" And, you come forward. Does Jesus say anything to you? Do you say anything to him? As Jesus is about to leave, he says, "Your faith has made you well." How do you feel when you hear these words? . . .

Now it is time to head for home. Take a moment to envisage your future now that you are well. What sort of life awaits you? What adventures lie ahead? . . .

Conclude with a moment of thanksgiving for God's transforming touch. . . .

Reflections of the community

Prayers of thanksgiving and intercession

Laying on of hands and anointing

Sending forth

A SERVICE OF HEALING AFFIRMATIONS

The Apostle Paul proclaimed, "Do not be conformed to this world, but be transformed by the renewing of your minds" (Romans 12:2). Our attitudes and beliefs radiate throughout our bodies. Our faith can be the tipping point between health and illness. Jesus' own ministry affirms that a new way of looking at ourselves and the world can bring healing to our bodies.

Affirmations are positive statements about ourselves and the world. The regular repetition of these healing words brings changes, first, to the conscious mind and, then, to the unconscious. In so doing, our thoughts may even change what neurophysiologists such as Candace Pert have described as the "molecules of emotion" present throughout the body.[15]

A service of healing affirmations seeks to transform our way of seeing ourselves and God's presence in our lives. Affirmations do not deny the pain and tragedy of life but place them in a wider, healing perspective. Living by positive, healing affirmations opens up new avenues for the interplay of divine energy and human agency.

A SERVICE OF THANKSGIVING AND AFFIRMATION

Words of affirmation   Romans 12:1–2;
                              1 Corinthians 6:19–20

("Do not be conformed to this world, but be transformed by the renewing of your minds." "Your body is the temple of the Holy Spirit. . . . Glorify God in your body.")

Silent prayer

Words of affirmation   Philippians 4:8–9

("Whatever is true, whatever is honorable . . . think about these things. . . . and the God of peace will be with you.")

Silent reflection

Healing affirmations from scripture[16]

Sharing the affirmations from scripture

Prayerful affirmation   Philippians 4:19

("My God will fully satisfy every need of yours according to [God's] riches in glory in Christ Jesus.")

Prayers of intercession

(Following each sentence, a moment for silence or shared intercessions.)

God of infinite love, remind us that we are your beloved daughters and sons. Awaken us to your dream for our lives. We affirm your blessing for all persons who are struggling with:

Life-threatening and chronic illness . . .

The pain of emotional, physical, or sexual abuse . . .

Grief at the loss of a loved one . . .

Illnesses of spirit, mind, or emotions . . .

The nearness of death . . .

Living with poverty and hunger . . .

Imprisonment for their political beliefs . . .

Terror of the future . . .

We place them in your hands, as we affirm your dream of abundance for all creation. We trust that your abundant life will supply all our needs.

Let our words of prayer create a healing environment . . . for ourselves . . . for those for whom we pray . . . for those who minister to body, mind, and spirit . . . for our nation's friends and enemies . . . and for our planet.

Let our lives mediate your healing touch to those in need of comfort or cure. Open our eyes to your dream for our lives and inspire us that we might work tirelessly as your healing partners. In the name of Christ. Amen.

The laying on of hands

> Jesus said, "I have come that [you] may have life, and have it abundantly." As we lay hands on you, I invite you to open to God's abundant life. Let God's healing energy flow through you, bringing healing of mind, body, spirit, and relationships.
>
> May God open our imagination to new possibilities to embody your reign in our world. In the name of Jesus of Nazareth, God's healing is yours.

Healing circle

> *(Each person around the circle is blessed as her or his name is mentioned.)*

Benediction

A SERVICE OF *LECTIO DIVINA* AND HEALING TOUCH

The practice of *lectio divina*, or holy reading, opens us to the healing of persons and communities. As we listen to scriptures, we awaken to God's intimate and personal healing word for us today. In the sharing of God's healing word in the community of faith, we gain insights into our own healing and, in the words of theologian Nelle Morton, hear each other into speech.[17] This service, like the Taizé service, joins prayer, sharing, and silence. In combination with laying on of hands, holy reading becomes wholly reading, words soothe wounds and enliven the "molecules of emotion."

The practice of *lectio divina* in a healing service or individual spiritual formation involves the following elements:

1. Slow reading of the appointed scripture;

2. Silence;

3. A second reading of the scripture;

4. Silent reflection;

5. Response to the following questions: What healing word or image do I hear in the scripture? What would it mean to embody this word in my life?;

6. Sharing in community.

The healing service follows a simple pattern in its emphasis on the healing power of scripture and sharing.

A HEALING SERVICE IN THE SPIRIT OF THE BENEDICTINE TRADITION

Greeting

Hymn

Silence

Lectio divina[18]

Sharing the word with one another

Prayer of thanksgiving

Prayers of intercession

Laying on of hands and anointing

Closing prayer

HEALING AND MEDICINE

Today, many congregations have established congregational health or parish nursing ministries that include healing touch, reiki, and therapeutic touch as well as preventative health care screening, health education, advocacy, and pastoral visitation. In some cases, these congregations join healing prayer with complementary health care services. Following the liturgical healing service, those who wish may receive healing touch treatments or seated massage. As the liturgical service concludes, persons who have expressed interest in healing treatments typically adjourn to a suite of private rooms for another form of laying on of hands.

In addition, virtually everyone who asks for healing prayer and laying on of hands is currently receiving Western medical care in the form of medication, surgery, chemotherapy, radiation, or physical therapy. Today's healing services, especially in congregations in which physicians and nurses are in attendance, can bridge the divide between technological and complementary medicine.

A number of factors are necessary for the successful integration of complementary and traditional Western medicine into the healing ministry of a congregation. Some of these are educational, while others are professional and architectural. It is especially helpful if the congregation provides appropriate educational preparation in the area of complementary and traditional Western health care. Indeed, many congregations provide "health fairs" that include blood pressure screening, information about mammograms and prostate screening, workshops in diet and exercise, and workshops in meditation for spiritual growth and stress reduction, along with seated massage, healing touch, and reiki. In the spirit of John's gospel, wherever truth and healing are experienced, God is its source. Although Jesus provided no methodology of healing, he healed persons by a variety of means, including touch, the mediation of healing energy, healing words, and distant prayer. Some of the techniques Jesus employed are now utilized by complementary health care practitioners as well as Western nurses and physicians. Many complementary approaches to health are not tied to a specific metaphysical system and can be adapted to the life of the church in the same way that secularized Western medicine can and should be utilized by church members.

Today's Christians can be educated in seeing the continuity between the healing touch of Jesus and today's complementary and technological healing modalities. Since countless mainstream and progressive Christians receive healing touch, reiki, massage, acupuncture, osteopathy, homeopathy, chiropractic, or ayurvedic health care, along with allopathic care, it is important for a church truly committed to healing ministry to weave complementary and technological health practices with its understandings of worship and theology. Today's congregations are called to build bridges that join, rather than walls that divide, Christian faith with the many complementary and technological practices available today.

Congregations that include complementary and technological health care as well as liturgical healing services in their healing ministries must also provide safe and attractive spaces where healing ministry teams can work. Two concerns are essential for any complementary healing or spiritual formation ministry—privacy and responsible community. On the one hand, sacred spaces need to be created where persons can comfortably relax. Second, each recipient needs to be treated in a safe and gentle healing fashion. Each person's unique attitude toward touch and personal space needs respect in a professional manner. In a time when many persons are the victims of physical, emotional, or sexual abuse or post-traumatic stress, congregations need to set guidelines for appropriate touch, record keeping, and confidentiality. In addition, they may need to provide professional insurance for healing practitioners. Congregational healing ministry is best done when teams of two provide appropriate comfort, care, and community.

While the integration of liturgical healing services and medical care can be done in a variety of ways, I suggest the following approach:

A Service of Healing Integrating Laying on of Hands and Health Ministry

Greeting	John 10:10 ("I came that [you] may have life, and have it abundantly.")
Hymn	
Scripture	

Silence

Group sharing

Pastoral meditation

Prayers of thanksgiving and intercession

Laying on of hands and anointing

Hymn

Closing prayer

Invitation

> *(Persons are invited to experience the many dimensions of healing following the formal service. They may either recess to the healing ministry center for healing treatments or make a future appointment. They may also take a moment for blood pressure screening or, in the autumn, this service can be held in the context of administering—in an adjoining room—flu shots to the congregation and the larger community.*
>
> The continuity of the healing ministry of Jesus and Western and complementary approaches needs to be expressed both in the pastor's words and in print materials such as bulletins and flyers. The heart of any bridge building ministry with complementary health care is the affirmation that "wherever truth and healing occur, God is its source, even if it comes from another culture." Accordingly, participants are encouraged to utilize the best resources in complementary and Western medicine along with spiritual formation and laying on of hands.)

A HEALING EUCHARIST

The celebration of communion has always been a medium of divine healing. In the sharing of the bread and the cup, we affirm God's creative love, embodied in the immense journey of the universe; the planetary journey of mountain, sea, and sky, and all who dwell therein; the human spiritual journey of wise women and men, prophets, Sunday school teachers, mentors, and pastors; and the life, teaching, death, and resurrection of Jesus the healer. The celebration of communion affirms that God dwells in human flesh—in Jesus of Nazareth—and in touch that heals mind, body, and spirit. In our prayers, we affirm that God's love heals sickness, abuse, racism, sexism, and oppression. Everything can be brought before God in the Supper that opens our eyes to Christ's presence and allows God to touch our deepest pain with holy love.

Today, many seekers, especially women and those who have been emotionally, sexually, and theologically abused or neglected, struggle with traditional understandings of communion. Too often the sacrifice of Christ has been interpreted in terms of the doctrine of substitutionary atonement and the satisfaction of divine anger at humankind or the restoration of God's honor. While the images of Jesus dying for our sins and taking on the burden of our guilt can be life-transforming for certain persons, we must articulate these images—if we use them at all —in ways that affirm God's infinite love for Jesus and ourselves. The cross is not divine child abuse, but the revelation of God's suffering love for humankind and all creation. God did not will Jesus' death, but worked within Jesus' pain and abandonment to bring new love and life to the world. Following Jesus does not require us to sacrifice ourselves but to claim God's abundant life and embody God's dream for ourselves and our world. While this may mean sacrifice for some persons, claiming God's love may also mean self-affirmation for others.

For some Christians such as Rebecca Ann Parker, president of Starr-King School of Religion in Berkeley, California, the sacrificial elements of communion only intensify the pain they experienced as sexually abused children. We cannot measure the pain that poorly articulated theology has brought to innocent victims. As Rebecca Ann Parker relates:

Even before I began to recover memories of having been sexually molested I decided to stop taking communion. I remember
one Sunday sitting in the back of the church when the words of
the communion liturgy were being read. An overwhelming feeling came over me that I had to get out of the sanctuary. The
place felt dangerous. The idea that the sacrifice of somebody
was a good idea, to be praised, suddenly felt directly threatening
to me.[19]

Holy and healing communion proclaims that we are not
called to bear the cross of Christ in our time. Jesus' sacrifice was
freely chosen and, because of Jesus' love, we do not have to sacrifice ourselves in abusive and disempowering life situations.
Indeed, the celebration of communion calls us to claim God's
healing in our lives and embrace God's gifts of self-discovery,
vocation, and adventure.

The following service of Holy Communion celebrates God's
universal, healing, and life-giving revelation. God's suffering
with us frees us from needless suffering and calls us to face our
pain knowing that God is with us and desires that we have
abundant life. God's aim is for each creature's self-actualization
in light of the well-being of this good earth. Creation and
humankind groan together, as the apostle Paul notes, as we
seek the wholeness God seeks for all things.[18]

HEALING COMMUNION

Invitation   John 15:5, 7

"I am the vine, you are the branches. Those who abide in me
and I in them bear much fruit, because apart from me you can
do nothing. . . . If you abide in me, and my words abide in
you, ask for whatever you wish, and it will be done for you."

We gather to celebrate the Love that brought us into life and guides us each step of the way. We gather in remembrance of Jesus the healer who mediated God's healing touch to the broken, lost, and lonely. Jesus' life, healing ministry, teaching and preaching, and death and resurrection, reveal that God is on our side. God feels our pain, heals our wounds, and gives us new life when death surrounds us.

God's love embraces each one of us and excludes none of us. In Christ's name, we invite anyone who seeks God's healing touch to share in this meal of reconciliation, transformation, healing, and love. As you share in the bread and the cup, let God's love flow in and through you, bringing healing and wholeness of body, mind, spirit, and relationships to yourself and those for whom you pray.

Eucharistic prayer

Pastor: God be with you.

People: And also with you.

Pastor: Let us open our hearts to God.

People: In wonder and awe, we claim God's love and are made whole through bread, wine, and healing touch.

Pastor: Let us give thanks to God.

People: For Healing Love is infinite and everlasting.

Pastor: We give you thanks, God of all creation, for your infinite love and creativity, and for your touch that makes us whole. You are the heart of all creation, and in your Holy Love, we joyfully live, move, and have our being. Your Beauty and Wisdom bring forth worlds without number.

Your Artistry brings forth the earth in all its diversity and wonder, and colors all living things. Your artistry gives us life and beauty. Your Holy Adventure guides the evolving universe and inspires our own personal adventures.

All creation breathes your spirit.

All creatures reflect your love.

Your Adventurous Love is heard in the cries of babies.

It inspires the voices of prophets, wise women and wise men.

It whispers in the everyday words of women and men of every tradition and time. It breathes through our pain and celebration.

In Original Wholeness, we are created in your image.

Your Beauty is our deepest identity.

As your beloved sons and daughters, our most basic essence is Holy Love.

We give you thanks, Intimate Creator, for the Wisdom Incarnate in in Jesus of Nazareth, the healer and lover, our faithful guide in our journey with You.

In Christ, we celebrate your gift of open vision and gentle power that reclaims the wholeness that is your intention for all things.

In Christ, all wounds are healed, all sin forgiven, all alienation reconciled.

In Christ, all suffering is cherished and transformed.

Let your Healing Spirit, O Loving Companion, break forth in our voices, as we and all creation, give voice to the sighs too deep for words.

All: **Holy, holy, holy Love.**

Heaven and earth are full of your glory.

Everything resonates with your touch.

With joy, we embrace your care that creates and responds.

We celebrate with all creation your healing touch.

In Christ, your tender strength is revealed.

You have brought Love to life, and Life to love.

You give us your peace.

Pastor: We remember your infinite love for all creation, revealed in Christ's love for us.

In the midst of suffering, love is victorious.

In the midst of woundedness, there is hope.

In the midst of death, new life springs forth.

In Christ's death and resurrection, in the bread and wine, our suffering is transformed, and our wounds are healed.

In sharing Christ's bread and wine, all meals, all touch, is made holy.

As our bodies and relationships are made whole, your loving promise is fulfilled.

All: **Let your Spirit transform our lives as we share in the bread and wine.**

Inspired by your embodied presence, we become healing partners and and co-creators in your Holy Adventure. Let your love heal us in word and touch, in silence and prayer, and call us to heal others.

Pastor: God's grace is embodied in bread and wine. God's healing gifts are for all of us.

Sharing the Bread and the Cup

Prayer After Communion

We thank you, O God, for the love that makes us whole. Receiving your grace, we vow to share your grace with others. As you touch us, we touch others in healing and love. In Christ's name. Amen.

Laying on hands and anointing with oil

Healing Circle

Blessing for the journey

chapter five

The Healed Healer

*A s soon as they left the synagogue, they entered the house
of Simon and Andrew, with James and John. Now
Simon's mother-in-law was in bed with a fever, and they told
him about her at once. He came and took her by the hand and
lifted her up. Then the fever left her and she began to serve
them. That evening, at sundown, they brought to him all who
were sick or possessed with demons. And the whole city was
gathered around the door. And he cured many who were sick
with various diseases, and cast out many demons; and he
would not permit the demons to speak, because they knew
him. In the morning, while it was still very dark, he got up and
went out to a deserted place, and there he prayed. And Simon
and his companions hunted for him. When they found him,
they said to him, "Everyone is searching for you." He
answered, "Let us go on to the neighboring towns, so that I
may proclaim the message there also; for that is what I came
out to do." (Mark 1:29–35)*

I regularly lead seminars on ministerial wholeness to new pastors serving in their first ministerial call. Over the years, I have
asked these idealistic and committed pastors to evaluate their
overall health in the years following seminary. The results of
my queries have been startling, to say the least. Malcolm, a

forty-year-old second career United Methodist pastor, confessed, "I feel like I'm on a treadmill. I go from task to task and crisis to crisis, and barely have an opportunity to reflect on my ministerial goals. The congregation is happy with my work. But, my wife and children are growing impatient with my evening meetings and emergency hospital visits. I'm working more these days than I did when I was an accountant." Sally, also in her forties and serving a Presbyterian (USA) congregation, describes her personal life in bleak terms, "My health and relationships have gone downhill since seminary. Even though I was working part-time during seminary, I still could focus on my prayer life and theological studies. I feel guilty because my prayer life is in shambles and I haven't read a serious theological text in the past six months. How can I be the spiritual leader of my congregation if I have no spiritual life myself?" In her first call following seminary, Georgia sees her life as United Church of Christ pastor as a physical and spiritual roller coaster: "I work like hell for a month, then predictably, I get sick. It's the only way I can get any rest. My congregation is talking about initiating a health ministry and healing service. But, how can I initiate a healing ministry, when I don't take care of myself? I would feel like a hypocrite!"

The words of these dedicated and skilled new pastors echo throughout the American church. Seasoned pastors of large and successful congregations also experience burnout and stress-related illness. Overwhelmed by the many tasks required of today's ministers, many self-medicate, disengage from their families, or engage in inappropriate pastoral behavior. While once the tasks of a pastor were primarily spiritual, homiletical and liturgical, today's pastors find their job descriptions vague and amoebic—Sunday preacher and liturgist, Christian educator, evangelist, CEO, building manager, pastoral counselor, spiritual guide, janitor, youth minister, and cheerleader. Many pastors live from crisis to crisis and, like Jesus' friend Martha, they are anxious about many things as they go from task to task with little opportunity for reflection or relaxation. Prayer, meditation, and personal well-being are all too easily neglected as unimportant compared to the daily demands of ministry. Without a spiritual center and the help of spiritual disciplines around which to prioritize the many demands of ministry, these pastoral leaders often lose their sense of mission and vocation. Like Georgia, they panic when they must preach on the healing passages in the lectionary or are asked to help initiate a congregational health program. "How can I preach about Jesus' healing ministry when I neglect my own well-being? How can I lead a prayer group when I don't pray myself?" many pastors confess. Yet, a ministerial crisis may be the opportunity for spiritual transformation when pastors allow their pain and burnout to awaken them to God's healing touch!

HEALING THE HEALERS

Ministry is profoundly incarnational in nature. While there is power and effectiveness in the office of ministry and the sacraments of the Christian church, the primary medium of healing ministry is the pastor, her- or himself. Healthy pastors shape their congregations in healthy and life-transforming ways. Unhealthy pastors do the opposite! They shape their congregations in unhealthy ways. Co-dependency is the most common problem. But, simple pastoral fatigue can lead to poor ethical judgment, boundary violations, betrayal of confidences, pastoral misconduct, and eventually burnout. Healthy ministry is a matter of the practical integration of theology, spiritual formation, discipline, and commitment.

Many pastors have internalized dysfunctional ministerial norms and destructive theological doctrines. Their lived images of God and themselves may differ radically from their formally stated theological positions. The gap is a dangerous one, not only for the pastor, but also for her or his congregation. Although Tom preached God's grace on Sunday mornings, his ministry was dominated by what Martin Luther described as "works righteousness." "If only I work harder and longer, my congregation will flourish and I will fulfill my vocation as pastor. If I take a holiday or don't answer the phone during my exercise time, I feel like I am betraying my call to ministry." Deep down, Tom worried that if he let down his guard and admitted his need for a sabbatical, he would be seen as a failure and lose his congregation's respect. He made constant last-minute revisions to his Sunday sermons. Though he was married with children, he was an absentee father and spouse from Saturday afternoon through coffee hour on Sunday morning, after which he collapsed. "They say you're only as good as your last sermon, and I believe it," Tom admitted. "If I don't wow them on Sunday, they may not come back next week." When he failed to find inspiration in scripture texts, Tom occasionally "borrowed" sermons off the internet. Near burnout and on the verge of separation from his wife, Tom sought the guidance of a spiritual friend. He was astounded and convicted when his spiritual friend noted, "If it's worth doing, it's worth doing badly." His spiritual guide continued, "What would happen if you preached a lousy sermon? Would they fire you? Would God turn away from you? Haven't you heard anything about grace after all these years of preaching about it?"

Anyone engaged in healing ministry, lay or ordained, needs to remember that healthy theology is grounded in the personal acceptance of God's surprising, unconditional, and unmerited grace. Although we constantly resist God's grace, believing we must earn our salvation, God's grace is relentless. In each moment of life, God offers us a vision of what we can be and the power to achieve it. This affirmation is at the heart of all healing. Grace is the gift of connectedness to God and the universe. Grace reminds us of the profound and holy interdependence that sustains us moment by moment.

So it was that one day, as he was reading Romans 8, Tom had an epiphany. When Paul wrote that nothing can "separate us from the love of God in Christ Jesus our Lord," he meant that nothing at all can keep God from loving us (Romans 8:38–39). Whether I fail or succeed in life, I am God's beloved child. Tom's theological epiphany transformed his mind, body, and relationships. Today, he still works hard, but also takes time for prayer, meditation, exercise, and family. While once he set his alarm for 3 a.m. on Sunday mornings, now he sleeps until 6:30 a.m. and, after a full Sunday schedule, still has the energy to play baseball and basketball with his sons and take a walk with his wife. Much to his surprise, Tom's pastoral relations committee has complimented him on improvements in his preaching and worship leadership! Even more surprising, the church board approved his request for a sabbatical and supported his idea to take off the fifth Sunday of the month as well as the weeks following Christmas and Easter.

Grace reminds us that we live, move, and have our being as God's beloved daughters and sons. Sadly, many pastors are lone rangers. They think we are indispensable and go it alone. Susan called herself "the queen of pastoral care." A spiritual ambulance chaser, she sometimes arrived at the hospital before her parishioners! She spent nearly every afternoon and evening making pastoral calls. When she admitted to her clergy women's support group that she was "bone weary," they challenged her to abdicate her throne and let her parishioners take greater responsibility for pastoral care. While it took several months for Susan to wean herself from her need to be present at every event, she eventually handed over the primary responsibility for non-emergency and nursing home pastoral care to the newly-created Stephen Ministry program in her congregation. Looking back on her own personal transformation, Susan now recognizes that if she had not relinquished the title of "queen of pastoral care," her congregation would never have started its now successful Stephen Ministry and congregational health and healing programs. "My letting go enabled others to become leaders in the congregation. I had been so busy being *the* minister that I failed to see that my church was blessed with dozens of capable lay ministers."

The gospels note that even *Jesus chose not to be everyone's pastor all the time.* In Luke's account of Jesus' journey to a deserted place, the gospel writer notes that:

> The crowds were looking for him; and when they reached him, they wanted to prevent him from leaving them. But he said to them, "I must proclaim the good news of the kingdom of God to the other cities also; for I was sent for this purpose." (Luke 4:42–43)

The people wanted Jesus to be their own personal chaplain and to set up a tabernacle in Capernaum. Imagine their disappointment and anger when Jesus said, "No." I believe that Jesus' "no" to the people was motivated by his own sense of spiritual affirmation. In saying "no" to the demands of his adoring congregation, Jesus said "yes" to those who would succeed him as spiritual leaders in Capernaum. He also said "yes" to his vocation as preacher of the reign of God throughout the country.

As you look at your own life, where do you need to say "no?" For us, the question may not be, "What would Jesus do?" but what would Jesus *not* do? Jesus knew he couldn't be on duty twenty-four hours a day. He went to a deserted place to pray to refresh his spirit and reconnect with his Parent's vision for his ministry. Perhaps Jesus struggled with his own indispensability. Yet, in moments of quiet, he gained insight and perspective into the nature of his calling as the revealer of God's reign of shalom.

Healing ministry is a marathon, not a sprint. What spiritual values do you need to affirm in order to be an effective minister for the long haul?

Healing ministry is also grounded in a transformational understanding of the pastor's vocational life. While ordained ministers are set apart for certain unique tasks in the life of the church, it is important that we recognize that every Christian has a calling to ministry. Ministry is the work of a community and not a single person. Within the intricate and dynamic body of Christ, every one has a gift—indeed, many gifts—for the health and well-being of the community of faith. These gifts, like the members of our congregations and ourselves, are always growing and changing, and to stay healthy our ministerial practice and identity must also grow and change.

Today, Craig looks back on his earlier understanding of vocation with humor as well as sadness. "When I was sixteen, I experienced the call to ministry. Like Samuel, I heard God call my name and felt a sense of mission—to share the good news of salvation. From that time on, my primary identity was being a minister. In seminary, I excelled in theology and preaching. I took a small country church and commuted 50 miles every Friday to make calls and lead worship on Sunday morning. Even after I married and had children, I knew I had only one vocation—preaching, teaching, and healing. Everything went well until I realized that I was a stranger in my own household. My parishioners and associate pastors shared more of my life than my wife and children! My wife and children frowned and rolled their eyes every time dinner was interrupted by a small problem that I treated as if it were a crisis." Stunned and uncertain of what to do next, Craig went away for a weekend of prayer and devotional reading. As he read Brother Lawrence's *The Practice of the Presence of God*, Craig was astounded when the monk asserted that his work in the kitchen with everyone shouting and making demands was as holy to him as time spent in formal worship. As Craig notes, "At that moment, it dawned on me that although I was called by God to ministry, ordained ministry was not my only vocation—I was also called to be a loving father of three children, an attentive and supportive spouse to my wife, a loyal son to my parents and brother to my siblings. I was called to take care of my body and spiritual life. I was called to receive as well as give."

This was Craig's *kairos* moment. Now, he knows that his whole life is a vocation in which each moment and relationship reflects God's aim at beauty and love. While it took months for him to turn his life around, Craig now admits that he is now becoming an "ordinary mystic." "Once I thought spirituality involved only special moments like worship, communion, and pastoral care. Now I see spirituality embodied in the most ordinary activities—driving my daughter to school, holding hands with my wife, playing catch with my son, having a cup of coffee with a good friend."

Each of these pastors became a "healed healer" as a result of their commitment to wholeness in ministry. For each of them, healing is a lifelong process that must be affirmed one moment at a time. Each one has realized that healthy theology is grounded in the sense of God's presence in every moment of life and the profound interconnectedness of all things. Aware of life's interdependence, they have learned to receive as well as give. They have struggled to move from an isolated, unilateral, and hierarchical model of ministry to a partnership and relational model of ministry. They have trusted God to supply their needs and forgive their imperfections. While each of these pastors aims at excellence in ministry, they have also achieved wholeness in their personal lives. They have learned the art of being "dispensable" and their ministries have flourished as others have found their gifts for service. Their healthy habits have been the foundation for long-term effectiveness in ministry. Their parishioners see them as models of healthy living and lively spirituality rather than overworked and anxious caregivers. While I believe that pastoral wholeness is multi-dimensional and unique to each person, I also affirm that commitment to the following practices is essential for pastoral well-being and spiritual integrity:

1. prayer and contemplation;
2. Sabbath time;
3. care for the body;
4. intellectual growth;
5. healthy relatedness.

WHOLENESS IN MINISTRY

Our theology is reflected in our values and personal commitments. Healthy ministry involves our embodiment of God's grace through cultivating the spiritual practices that enable us to be God's healing partners. Our leadership in congregational health ministries and healing services depends on our own intimate connection with God. Connected to the Vine, we will bear much fruit and God's healing energy will flow not only through our words, but also through our silence and touch. While every pastor's spiritual path is personal and unique, I will outline a spirituality of wholeness for pastors and congregational leaders in the following paragraphs.

Contemplation in a world of action. The reading from Mark with which this chapter began portrays a "day in the life of Jesus." Like today's pastors, Jesus' average day involved many diverse tasks—preaching, teaching, healing, casting out demons, and having a business dinner with ministerial associates. Today's pastor must also multi-task. Just think of your day: a morning meeting at Starbucks with the evangelism chair, putting together the Sunday bulletin, writing an article for the church newsletter, dealing with a conflict over space between the director of the church's preschool and the chair of Christian education, lunch with a colleague, reading a commentary for Sunday's sermon, phoning a few shut-ins to make appointments for visits, a trip to the emergency room to meet a widower experiencing chest pains, a call from a judicatory official, and planning for an interfaith rally against racism. Yet, the healed healer also makes time to go to a deserted place to pray, especially on the busiest days.

Though she is pastor of a growing 400-member church, Anne begins the day with a time of centering prayer. She closes her eyes for fifteen minutes. Her repetitive prayer word awakens her to the still, small voice of God. When her mind wanders as it often does when she thinks of the many tasks ahead, she simply brings it back to her prayer word without judgment or anger. "I have learned that meditation is life and life is meditation," Anne affirms. Her practice of centering prayer not only relaxes her and lowers her blood pressure, but opens her to new insights about her many vocations as pastor, mother, and spouse. This time of quiet centers her and gives her a larger perspective on the events of the day. "Once I saw every pastoral conflict as an emergency, now I know that this too will pass. More and more, I am becoming the non-anxious presence that calms the storms of my congregation." When she feels the first waves of anxiety, Anne simply takes a deep breath and remembers her prayer word. In a moment or so, she regains her spiritual center along with her sensitivity and effectiveness as a pastor.

Profoundly extroverted, Frank can't sit down for prayer. But, each day, he puts on his head phones and laces up his running shoes for a mid-afternoon jog. "Sometimes I listen to Enya, other times to praise music or U-2. Still other times to jazz or symphonic music. As I listen to the music and jog through the neighborhood, I feast my eyes on the changing panorama. I always come back refreshed and renewed, and ready to respond to the next pastoral challenge."

Another extrovert, Holly chants her faith each morning and throughout the day. She has found the Taizé chants a wonderful way to center herself amid the many chores of ministry and family life. "I have become a kitchen mystic, and the centering I experience as I chant and clean stays with me all day long."

Holly admits that she often sings along with Taizé chants as she drives from one pastoral call to the other.

Samantha breathes her prayers. Inspired by Psalm 150, "Let everything that breathes, praise [God]," Samantha does a simple breath prayer each morning and then breathes deeply throughout the day. The chimes of her church remind her throughout the day to breathe the Spirit deeply regardless of what she is doing. Before she steps up to the pulpit each Sunday, she takes a few calming breaths to remind her that God will be speaking through her words to the congregation.

Steve combines reading the daily offices of the *Book of Common Prayer* with his daily devotional reading. "I try to read a bit of the church's liturgy in the morning before I leave for church, at midday, and before I leave for home. I take a few moments to pray the Compline service each evening before I retire as a way of letting go of the past and opening to the possibilities that will greet me upon rising in the morning. These prayers weave God's presence into every activity I do. They bring a sense of peace and unity to the ever-changing tasks of ministry."

Healthy ministry balances action and contemplation. In the midst of the challenges of social upheaval, the Psalmist counsels, "Be still, and know that I am God!" (Psalm 46:10). Kierkegaard once proclaimed that "purity of heart is to will one thing."[1] The one thing we do as healed healers is to give and receive Christ's love in every situation. Awakened to God's presence, we discover that all places and encounters are holy. Grounded in God's graceful interdependence, we realize that we don't have to do everything or succeed in every task we attempt in order to be faithful to our Creator. In gaining spiritual perspective, we discover the stamina and hope that enables us to commit ourselves to tasks that may not be realized in our tenure as pastor or lifetime as disciples.

Sabbath time. Our attitude toward time can be a matter of life and death, both physically and spiritually. Physicians have noted the impact of "hurry sickness" or "time sickness" as a factor in stress-related illness. Most modern people complain, on the one hand, about not having enough time, and yet, on the other hand, speak of "killing time" when they must wait at a medical appointment or for an air flight!

Think about your own attitude toward time: is time your friend or enemy? Are you constantly updating your PDA or date book? Do you struggle with double-booking or racing from one place to another like the white rabbit in Alice's Adventures in Wonderland? Healthy ministry requires a spacious and hospitable spirit. Ironically, if you gather a crowd of pastors together, sooner or later, they will vie with one another about how much they have to do and how stressed they feel. Like the secular world, they feel that their value will be judged primarily by their productivity, level of stress, and non-stop busy-ness.

While many Christians devalue the importance of Sabbath-keeping as a result of their unimaginative interpretations of Jesus' conflicts with certain Pharisees over his Sabbath healings, a closer reading of scripture reveals that Jesus took the Sabbath seriously as a time for worship, refreshment, and companionship. Jesus recognized that the interplay of divine creativity and human freedom requires moments of rest and recreation.

> And on the seventh day God finished the work that [God] had done, and [God] rested on the seventh day from all the work that [God] had done. So God blessed the seventh day and hallowed it, because on it God rested from all the work that [God] had done in creation. (Genesis 2:2–3)

Created in God's image, we find wholeness in the dynamic interplay of rest and activity. As Rabbi Abraham Joshua Heschel observes, the Sabbath creates a "sanctuary of time" that hallows the rest of the week.[2]

Remember the sabbath day, and keep it holy. Six days you shall labor and do all your work. But the seventh day is a sabbath to the Lord your God; you shall not do any work. (Exodus 20:8–10a)

For a number of years, our family lived near an Orthodox Jewish congregation in Potomac, Maryland. Every Saturday families, young and old, walked to the temple, gathered for celebratory meals, and spent time in study and play. They were a constant reminder to me that even if you love your work, spiritual and physical well-being requires that you pause awhile and turn from focusing on your own efforts to relying solely on God's grace.

Now, I must admit that Sabbath keeping is a challenge to me. As a seminary professor and administrator, writer, congregational pastor, and visiting speaker, Sunday has almost always been a work day. Saturday has typically been a day of domestic chores and preparation for Sunday. I love what I do, but I have come to realize that if I am to live a balanced and healthy life in body, mind, spirit, and relationships, I must turn off the computer, put my pen down, forego another pastoral call or administrative memo, and simply relax in God's presence. For me, the Sabbath is a profound act of trust. In letting go of my own agenda, I trust God's care for the universe, my family, my work, and myself. In the spirit of Jesus' description of the birds of the air and the lilies of the field, I spend the day with activities that neither "toil nor spin."

Jesus' healing ministry reminds us that we need to be flexible with our Sabbath keeping and self-care. Even on our day of rest, we may have to spring into action if a parishioner is dying or has a personal crisis. Still, keeping a spiritual Sabbath, at least for one or two afternoons each week, must take priority over the trivialities that often overwhelm the pastor. The healed healer takes time to rest, study, and share with her or his friends and family. Even if we cannot take a literal twenty-four-hour Sabbath, health and wholeness require time apart, dedicated to refreshing the spirit. Spiritual guide Tilden Edwards has called such times Sabbath moments—momentary withdrawals from doing and achieving in order to reconnect with God, our deepest self, and those around us.[3] In dedicating a morning or afternoon to receive God's grace in friendship, rest, and study, we discover the meaning of Heschel's affirmation: "The Sabbath surrounds you wherever you go."[4]

For those involved in healing ministries, Sabbath keeping is a way to consciously reconnect with the spiritual resources of the Divine Vine. Trusting God to supply us with the energy, inspiration, and security that we need to flourish, our lives become fruitful reflections of God's life-giving abundance (John 15:1–11).

Too often, pastors rush back from appointments and calls to lead the midweek healing service. Already anxious and stressed-out, they find it difficult to listen to the needs of others. Caught up in their own agenda, they neglect God's "sighs too deep for words." Their own busy-ness contributes to an atmosphere of haste and anxiety rather than an environment of rest, calm, and peace that is necessary for contemplative, healing leadership. Accordingly, I suggest that prior to the healing service, the pastor take a mini-Sabbath—an hour or so for a walk in the neighborhood, a time of prayerful contemplation, a refreshing moment with an inspirational text—as a means of opening to God's healing energy. Renewed and refreshed, we will be energetic channels of blessing to those for whom we pray.

Glorifying God with our bodies. How we treat our bodies is a spiritual and ethical as well as physical issue. The apostle Paul challenges the Corinthian Christians to see their bodies as the "temple of the Holy Spirit within you" and to "glorify God" in their bodies (1 Corinthians 6:19–20). In contrast to Paul's wholistic vision of human life, many pastors, despite their theological orthodoxy, are closet Gnostics who neglect their physical well-being and deny the importance of diet and lifestyle in the conduct of their ministries.

Just listen to their stories. Georgia confesses, "I want to exercise, but I just don't have the time. Whenever I want to exercise, the phone rings and off I go on another pastoral visit. When I look at myself in the mirror or feel the tension rising, I know I need to mend my ways." A pastor of a central Pennsylvania congregation, Steve affirms that "ministry and overeating go hand in hand. Everywhere I go, there are pastries and snacks. When I make a pastoral call, there is always pie and coffee. And, when I get home, after a hard day, I need two cocktails and some chips and dip just to relax."

The integrity of our healing ministries depends on our care for our physical as well as spiritual lives. Our care of our bodies is just as much an issue of stewardship as our finances and talents. While a healthy lifestyle cannot always prevent chronic illness, cancer, or heart disease, healed healers must "walk the walk" as well as "talk the talk" in their commitment to physical, emotional, and relational well being. Glorifying God in our bodies means a commitment to physical exercise, healthy diet, and adequate rest.

A commitment to physical exercise is essential to physical, emotional, and spiritual well-being. We are made for movement as well as rest. Even fifteen minutes of moderately-paced walking three times a week reduces stress, enhances the immune system, and increases metabolic functioning. Until my mid forties, I jogged three miles each morning. Now in my early fifties, I take a brisk three mile prayer walk at sunrise and another in the early evening. During these daily walks, I feast my eyes on the beauty of trees and skies, reflect on scriptures, breathe my prayers, and sometimes simply enjoy the joys of fluid motion. I try to walk with my wife several times a week. Our walks give us time to share our hopes, dreams, and challenges; talk out relational issues; or simply hold hands. Our walks together remind us that a loving marriage involves an ongoing relational journey in which we travel together toward a shared vision. Other pastors balance their commitment to prayer with a daily regimen of jogging, swimming, cycling, yoga, Pilates, or Tai Chi. Moving in the spirit awakens us to God's presence in every cell of our bodies and affirms the goodness and beauty of our own human flesh. Most pastors echo the words of Peter, "My commitment to a regular program of exercise and stress-reduction is the only thing that gets me through days filled with unexpected hospital visits and administrative crises. Sometimes after a long day, I take a fifteen-minute run. In that short run, the stresses and worries of the day roll off my back. I return home with a sense of peace and happiness that enables me to be a good husband and father the rest of the evening."

Biblical faith affirms the importance of diet. Our relationship with God is reflected in the food we eat and our generosity toward the hungry and vulnerable. While no one diet fits all persons, it is important for pastors to watch what they eat since much of our work involves meetings and pastoral calls, often accompanied by finger foods, snacks, or meals. I must admit that I am easily lured by a doughnut at a midmorning meeting even though I have just finished my low-carbohydrate breakfast. I delight in the taste of cheese cake and cherry pie and enjoy a celebratory cookout with friends. As pastors, we are not called to be ascetics, but to be wise stewards in our eating and drinking. The key both to diet and exercise is to find a path that gives you joy and supports your well-being. It is also important for some of us to discern why we overeat and seek gentle but assertive support in transforming our attitudes toward food. The goal is not an "extreme pastoral makeover" but enough energy and wellness for good ministry, lively relationships, and everyday adventures. As we explore new attitudes toward food and exercise, it goes without saying that we need to seek the advice of our physician or other health care giver.

The healing ministry of Jesus reminds us of the transforming power of touch. Jesus' touch energized, welcomed, and healed persons in their vulnerability. Jesus knew that mind and body interpenetrate one another and that an affirmative touch could bring wholeness to a person's spirit as well as body. While many persons suffer from unholy touch, loving and welcome touch can be a major factor in spiritual and physical wellness. In describing the importance of touch, philosopher Ashley Montagu asserted that next to the brain, the skin is the most important of our organ systems.[4] Without healthy touch, infants wither and die. As adults, we also need hugs from friends, gentle caresses, and supportive healing touch.

Today, many pastors have experienced the healing power of massage, reiki, and therapeutic touch. Healing touch energizes, connects, balances, and enhances physical, emotional, and spiritual well-being. In an attempt to support the well-being of parish pastors, the pastoral leadership renewal program at Lancaster Theological Seminary provides seated massage and yoga along with classes in theological reflection, preaching, and spiritual formation. Andover Newton Theological School has initiated a Center for Faith, Health, and Spirituality, which includes reiki treatments and trainings as part of its wellness program.[6] In allowing others to touch our bodies lovingly, our own bodily attitudes change and we learn to love God in the world of the flesh, and most especially our own bodies.

Holy relationships. The philosopher Alfred North Whitehead once noted that the whole universe conspires to create each moment of experience. Relationship is the nature of all life, human and non-human. As Genesis proclaims, "it is not good that [humans] be alone" (Genesis 2:18). The "first" human's words in discovering a life partner affirm the nature of human relationships at their best—"'This at last is bone of my bones and flesh of my flesh.'" . . . [A]nd the man and the woman were both naked, and were not ashamed" (Genesis 2:23, 25). The biblical accounts of the origins of humankind are not about physiology or chronology, but holy relatedness. We are meant to be connected in loving relationships.

In describing his vision of the church, the apostle Paul speaks of Christian community as the "body of Christ," an intricately woven community of communities in which our joys and sorrows are one. Sadly, human relatedness is one of the primary victims of unhealthy ministry. Aaron was rocked to the core when his wife demanded that he spend more time with her and their children or she would leave the marriage. "I was so dedicated to the church that I forgot loving my family was also a spiritual calling," Aaron now admits.

A United Methodist pastor, Sandra tells of an encounter with her twelve-year-old daughter one evening following the Sunday night youth group meeting. Her daughter complained, "I wish I were in the high school group, then you would spend time with me." From that moment on, Sandra vowed to spend as much time with her kids as with the children of the church. Healthy ministry is grounded in healthy relationships beyond the congregation. A healthy life involves intimate relationships with spouses, partners, good friends, and colleagues. We are called to reach out beyond ourselves in relationships grounded in creative and intimate giving and receiving. Plato noted that a philosopher without love is dead, and the same truth applies to ministry. Loving relationships challenge, nurture, and revitalize ministry. They call us to examine how we relate to others and invite us to move beyond childhood relational patterns to creative and mutual relationships. In exploring our relationships, we may discover that we need the companionship of a ministerial support group or a spiritual guide or therapist as we seek the healing of our emotional, relational, and vocational lives.

While it is not my intent to provide guidelines for healthy relationships, it is clear that without healthy and egalitarian relationships outside the church, ministers will eventually be unable to relate in healing ways to their parishioners. Just as there are many paths to healing, there are varieties of healing relationships. For some, it is the give and take of a committed, growing, equal, and faithful marriage or holy union. For other persons, it is a close spiritual friendship with a non-romantic companion or soul friend who mirrors God's presence in our life. Still others find wholeness in healthy collegial relationships that integrate theological reflection, spiritual formation, and intimate sharing. Today, many programs—such as Lancaster Theological Seminary's Wholeness in Ministry program for new pastors, the Alliance for the Renewal of Ministry program for experienced pastors, and Harvesting Wisdom for pastors considering retirement or recently retired—offer pastors a safe place for exploring their own healing and wholeness along with theological reflection and leadership renewal.

Once again, Jesus' own ministry provides a model for healthy relationships. In his relationships with Mary, Martha, Mary of Magdala, and Lazarus, Jesus took time for receiving as well as giving love, for good food and drink, and for laughter and story telling. In the spirit of the healer Jesus, our own sensitivity to others' healing journeys is heightened and transformed through our sustained commitment to loving relationships.

Loving God with your mind. Luke's gospel proclaims that Jesus "grew in wisdom and in [stature], and in divine and human favor." (Luke 2:52)[7] Wisdom is the gift of experiencing the divine in the ordinary moments of life as well as the ability to see life from the perspective of eternity. Stature involves our ability to embrace as much of reality as possible without losing our own spiritual center.

Healing ministry finds its inspiration in a commitment to intellectual transformation. On the one hand, pastors who are committed to leading healing services must research the best resources on Jesus' healing ministry, the healing ministry of the church throughout history, contemporary healers, and the interplay of spirituality, Western medicine, and complementary medicine. As the theologians of their congregations, pastors must be bridge builders between spirituality and medicine, whether it is Western or complementary. Further, their understanding of healing must be grounded in a lively and inspiring

Christian vision of reality. Accordingly, a glance at the healing pastor's study and bedside will reveal an assortment of texts on healing, theology, pastoral care, and spiritual formation. As theologian of her or his congregation, the pastor is called to respond seriously and sensitively to issues relating to the problem of evil, the randomness of illness and death, and our own role in health and illness. Committed to her or his own theological growth through study and continuing education, the pastor becomes a healing resource to persons facing life's most difficult challenges.

Still, beyond reading in theology and spiritual formation, today's pastors would do well to immerse themselves in good fiction and poetry as a means of liberating their imaginations as well as experiencing the pure joy of a good poem or book. Good fiction opens us to dimensions of the human adventure that are often hidden in theological and scientific literature. Poetry awakens us to new ways of perceiving reality as well as novel forms of sharing wisdom.

Finally, the pastor must take seriously the apostle Paul's challenge, "Do not be conformed to this world, but be transformed by the renewing of your minds" (Romans 12:2). Healthy mindfulness alerts us to our negative self-talk and destructive attitudes about ourselves and others. The creative use of affirmations not only heals our self-image and feelings of ineffectiveness but also transforms the unconscious mind if practiced over time.

At first, the use of affirmations may seem unrealistic and counterfactual. When we doubt the power of creative affirmations and imaginative visualizations to change our lives, we are reminded that many of Jesus' healings involved inspiring persons to see themselves in new and unexpected ways—as God's beloved children, worthy of God's healing touch and able to be partners in their own healing adventures.

While I regularly use affirmations in my sermon preparation, I have discovered the power of healing affirmations to support my own quest for wholeness. I have found the following affirmations helpful in my own journey in healing ministry. Each one is grounded in the biblical vision of God's empowering presence in our lives. Accordingly, affirmations are not merely self-talk but creative ways to experience God's inspiration in our lives and our essential identity as God's beloved children. Some helpful Christian affirmations include:

— I am the light of the world. (Matthew 5:14)

— My faith brings wholeness to my life. (Mark 5:34)

— God speaks to me in sighs too deep for words. (Romans 8:26)

— In all things God is working for good in my life. (Romans 8:28)

— Nothing can separate us from the love of God. (Romans 8:39)

— I open myself to divine transformation. (Romans 12:2)

— My body is the temple of God's spirit. (1 Corinthians 6:19)

— I glorify God with my body. (1 Corinthians 6:20)

— I rejoice in God's presence in my life. (Philippians 4:4)

— I can do all things through God who strengthens me. (Philippians 4:14)

— My God will supply all my needs. (Philippians 4:19)

Circles and boundaries. Do you remember the encounter of Naaman and Elisha? (2 Kings 5:1–19) When Elisha tells Naaman that he will be healed if he simply dips himself in the Jordan River, the general becomes angry. He expected something dramatic, complicated, and expensive, when the healer suggested the simplest and most straightforward action. Our own healing is often right in front of us as well. All we need to do—and this is frankly the hard part—is to follow the directions, manifest in the wisdom of body, mind, spirit, and relationships that flow in and through us by God's grace. Healing our ministries involves a commitment to caring for ourselves so that we can care for others.

Jesus' ministry shows us that wholeness in ministry involves circles that embrace and boundaries that affirm. In the course of a day in the life of Jesus, the healer embraced and welcomed the vulnerable as well as the powerful. His table was open to outcasts as well as insiders. Virtually every healing of Jesus transformed a person's place in society as well as her or his body and spirit. Yet, Jesus' ability to heal was grounded in his intimate relationship with the Healing and Creating God. In order to say "yes" to his mission as God's Beloved Son, Jesus had to say "no" to the unrealistic demands of the crowd. He also had to say "no" to the need to be on duty twenty-four hours a day so he could be fully present for persons in need of healing and acceptance.

The health of Jesus' ministry is revealed in the intimacy with God that enabled him to center on God's aim for healing in his life. As his journey in the wilderness reveals, Jesus was tempted early in his ministry to follow unhealthy spiritual patterns. But, in turning to God in times of temptation, he found the courage and power to follow God even when it meant suffering and death. The healer Jesus' final healing act may have been the most difficult—at the Ascension, Jesus let go of the need to control by entrusting the future of his ministry to his fallible followers.

Today, we are entrusted with Jesus' healing ministry. In following the healer of Nazareth, we are also called to integrate our embrace of the vulnerable and lost with an affirmation of our own commitment to personal, relational, and professional healing. Becoming a healed healer is a process and not the end of our spiritual journey. We must protect and affirm our well-being every day so that we might be clear and powerful channels of God's healing touch. Connected with God's healing presence as a result of our commitment to our own growth and health, our healing process enables us to be partners in God's infinite circle of healing.

chapter six

Education in Healing

*W*hen *it was evening that day, the first day of the week,
and the doors of the house where the disciples had met
were locked for fear of [some Jewish leaders], Jesus came and
stood among them and said, "Peace be with you." After he
said this, he showed them his hands and his side. Then the disciples rejoiced when they saw the Lord. Jesus said to them
again, "Peace be with you. As the [Parent] has sent me, so I
send you." When he said this, he breathed on them and said to
them, "Receive the Holy Spirit." . . . But Thomas (who was
called the twin), one of the twelve, was not with them when
Jesus came. So the other disciples told him, "We have seen the
Lord." But he said to them, "Unless I see the mark of the nails
in his hands, and put my finger in the mark of the nails and
my hand in his side, I will not believe." A week later his disciples were again in the house, and Thomas was with them.
Although the doors were shut, Jesus came and stood among
them and said, "Peace be with you." Then he said to Thomas,
"Put your finger here and see my hands. Reach out your hand
and put it in my side. Do not doubt but believe." Thomas
answered him, "My Lord and my God!"* (John 20:19–28)

The emergence of healing ministries in mainstream and progressive churches is the sign of a new Pentecost within Protestant
Christianity. For the first time in Christian history, congrega-

tions have the opportunity to join faith and science *and* medical technology and healing touch as essential aspects of their mission and ministry. The rise of dynamic healing ministries within mainstream and progressive churches is the result, first, of our openness to God's surprising movements in our lives and, second, of our willingness to face squarely the doubter within each one of us, while persisting in the struggle until—like the fabled and misunderstood apostle Thomas—we experience God's healing presence in our lives.

After thoughtful theological reflection and committed spiritual formation, many congregations plan healing services with the expectation that God will touch our lives in gentle and unanticipated ways. While we do not expect supernatural interruptions of the processes of nature, the dynamic vision of reality presented by scripture, quantum physics, and the emerging partnership of spirituality and medicine reminds us that within the interdependent matrix of mind, body, spirit, and relationships, holy touch and faithful prayer can bring unexpected wholeness to our lives.

Like the apostle Thomas, thoughtful Christians are invited to explore the healings of Jesus and the healing renewal of the church with all their questions and doubts. As we wrestle with questions and doubts raised by tension between the reality of sickness and the often dramatic healing narratives of the gospel, we may receive the blessing of a creative, inclusive, and growing healing ministry. No question is off limits, no doubt is stifled, for within our struggle to believe, we will discover the healing Christ.

Theological education is essential to a successful healing ministry. In spite of the sound-byte theology characteristic of many congregations and televangelists, we are called to love God with our minds as well as our hearts. A transformed mind can change our attitudes, awaken us to new possibilities for growth and adventure, and influence our physical well-being. A thinking church is a growing church that makes room for new visions of God and the world. As Abigail Rian Evans asserts, "Preparation for healing services involves several parts: education of the congregation, training of leaders and participants, and publicity."[1] Theological education, like spiritual growth, takes time, but the reward is great—building congregational life on the rock of deep, tested faith rather than instant and superficial answers. In this chapter, we will focus on the role of theological education and spiritual formation in establishing healing services and training an effective team of healing partners.

HEALING EDUCATION

Our theology shapes our vision of reality, ourselves, and God's presence in our lives. Creative theological reflection is profoundly practical in nature: it presents a vision of reality and provides a path to experience the realities it affirms. On the one hand, we need to challenge harmful images of God and human life that imply that sickness is entirely the result of divine punishment, God's will, or personal sin. We need to formulate healthy and life-supporting theological visions that are responsive to the many spiritually and physically wounded persons who come in need of God's healing touch. On the other hand, we need to affirm a constructive vision of God's healing presence in our lives. Constructive theology enables us to discern, albeit in a fragmentary way, how much we can expect of God and ourselves in the divine-human healing synergy. As children of the Enlightenment, we often expect too little from God in terms of God's ability to transform mind, body, and spirit. Further, our theological world views often limit our understanding of prayer to little more than individual or corporate self-talk. Such metaphysical humility prevents us from seeing the ordinary and extraordinary healings that are available in each moment of experience.

In the following paragraphs, I will present the broad outlines of an adventure in congregational healing that embraces theology, spiritual formation, worship, and pastoral care. At the heart of this adventure is the affirmation that each congregation will shape its curriculum and healing ministry in terms of its own unique gifts and challenges. In the spirit of Jesus' healings, this curricular adventure is grounded in compassion, empathetic listening, and loving responsiveness. Accordingly, participants are challenged to cultivate healing ears as well as healing hands. We must teach healing in a *healing* way by honoring doubts and questions, listening to pain and reticence, touching with care and compassion, and inspiring each person to experience their own healing relationship with God.

AN ADVENTURE IN CONGREGATIONAL HEALTH AND HEALING

WEEK ONE:
INTRODUCTION TO HEALING AND WHOLENESS

1. A time of silent and spoken prayer.

2. Explanation of the "healing adventure" that is beginning and the hope that the congregation will explicitly embark on the adventure of healing ministry.

3. Group sharing of hopes and expectations for the congregation's healing ministry. "When I hear the word healing, I think of _____."

4. Sharing of doubts, questions, and concerns regarding divine healing.

5. Mini-lecture: the revolution in healing and wholeness: the growing partnership of spirituality, Western medicine, and complementary medicine.

6. An experience in *lectio divina*: Luke 18:35–43 (the healing of a blind beggar)—see pages 87-88, 133-134.

7. Group sharing of *lectio divina*.

8. The weeks ahead—discovering the healings of Jesus and their meaning in our time.

9. Closing circle of intercession and blessing.

Week Two: The healings of Jesus I

1. Opening meditation: centering prayer—see page 134.

2. Group sharing: what are your favorite healing stories?

3. Group sharing: how did Jesus heal persons? What methods did he use?

4. Guided meditation on the woman with the flow of blood (Mark 5:25–34) – see pages 83-84.

5. Conversation on the guided meditation.

6. Mini-lecture: The relationship between faith and health: does faith make a difference?

   Scientific research on religious activity and the power of prayer.

   What if you don't get well? All the wrong answers!

7. Healing and touch: safe touch, energy and touch, laying on of hands and anointing.

8. Closing circle of prayer and anointing.

Week Three: The Healings of Jesus II

1. Meditation on God's healing light –see pages 135-136.

2. Mini-lecture: The relationship between healing and curing: a shalom approach to healing.

   While there may not be a cure, there can always be a healing.

3. *Lectio divina* on Luke 17:11–19 (the grateful Samaritan).

4. Group sharing.

5. The healing power of gratitude: "counting our blessings."

6. Body prayer: "I thank you God for the wonder of my being."

7. Closing circle of intercession and laying on of hands.

WEEK FOUR: GLOBAL HEALING

1. Breath prayer based on Psalm 150 ("let everything that breathes praise [God]")—see page 135.

2. Mini-lecture and discussion: The growing interest in complementary medicine.

   What types of complementary medicine have you used?

   Are there challenges in integrating complementary medicine and Christianity?

3. Mini-lecture: Christianity and Western medicine: joining "prayer and Prozac."

4. Group reflection: Wherever truth and healing are found, God is its source.

5. *Lectio divina* on Luke 7:1–10, "the healing of the Centurion's servant."

6. Group conversation.

7. Mini-lecture: Taking your medicine in a healing way.

8. A complementary healing ministry in the church?

9. Closing healing circle: healing in the light of God—light meditation for ourselves and others—see page 135-136.

WEEK FIVE: HEALING WORSHIP

1. Centering prayer.

2. The meaning of worship—ritual and sacraments.

   Your most meaningful worship experiences.

   The elements of healing worship. Exploring Isaiah 6:1–8.

3. *Lectio divina* on James 5:13–16.

4. Imaging a healing service in our congregation. What type of service would fit your theological, liturgical, and spiritual setting?

5. Group worship imagining and planning.

6. Concluding communion and laying on of hands.

WEEK SIX: HEALING AND THE COMMUNITY OF FAITH

1. Guided meditation on the body of Christ—see pages 136-137.

2. Healing and the mission of our congregation.

3. Healing and Sunday worship. Special healing services. When shall we have our healing services?

4. Healing and the church's health care ministry: parish nursing, congregational health ministry, advocacy for the vulnerable.

5. Conducting our congregation's life in a healing way: healing and administration, decision-making, and long-range planning.

6. Closing healing circle: praying for the healing of our congregation and its ministries.

WEEK SEVEN: HEALING THE PLANET

1. Centering prayer.

2. The reality of sin and pain in society and the planet.

3. *Lectio divina* on Luke 4:16–19 ("the Spirit of the Lord is upon me").

4. The Hebraic image of Shalom and the New Testament vision of the reign of God. The dream of "mending the world."

5. Group sharing: How can we be God's partners in mending the world?

Health as a social as well as personal matter.

Prayer and the transformation of the "powers and principalities."

Advocacy and action in social change.

Preventative care: responding to unhealthy social conditions.

The church's responsibility for "the least of these."

6. Meditation on healing ourselves and healing the planet.—see pages 137-138.

WEEK EIGHT: HEALING THE HEALERS

1. Guided meditation on "the storm at sea"—see pages 138-139.

2. The importance of becoming a healed healer.

3. The practices of health and wholeness:

    Exercise

    Sabbath time

    Meditation

    Diet

    Learning

    Healthy relationships

4. Where do we go from here?

    Forming a healing team.

    Further opportunities for study in our congregation.

    Scheduling the healing service?

    The next steps for our church.

5. Closing communion and laying on of hands.

PREPARING THE WAY IN PREACHING AND WORSHIP

In chapter two, we explored the importance of healing homilies. Since the Sunday service is the primary form of corporate theological reflection in congregational life, it is imperative that the pastor and the worship committee plan sermons and liturgies that include healing emphases as preparation for initiating an explicit healing ministry. On the one hand, the pastor may choose to preach a sermon series on the healings of Jesus that addresses the theological, spiritual, and practical issues surrounding healing in contemporary churches. A four to seven week series might include themes such as:

— The relationship between healing and faith (the woman with the flow of blood, Mark 5:25–34).

— The healing power of community (the man let down through the roof, Luke 5:17–26).

— God, pain, and suffering (the man born blind, John 9:1–7).

— Faith and medicine (the healing of a man's blindness, Mark 8:22–26).

— Christianity and complementary medicine (the disciples stifle another healer, Luke 9:49–50).

— Death and healing (the post-resurrection encounter of Jesus and Mary of Magdala, John 20:1–18).

— Healing the planet (Jesus preaches in Nazareth, "the spirit of the Lord is upon me," Luke 4:16–21).

Although the lectionary readings of the church provide an unfocused, ambient perspective of healing and wholeness, the insightful pastor can integrate healing themes within the three-year lectionary cycle. He or she may highlight issues of healing and wholeness when the gospel reading focuses on the healings of Jesus. Further, even scripture passages that do not directly address physical or spiritual healing may lend themselves to reflection on issues such as the healing of relationships and memories, self-care, the power of prayer, the role of God in our lives, and the interplay of social justice and personal well-being. In planning the worship service, the pastor and worship committee may complement the work of the healing study group by including intentional times of intercessory prayer and silence in the Sunday liturgy. These times can be prefaced by scriptures and theological reflections that affirm God's abiding and transforming presence in our lives. In addition, an insightful pastor and worship committee will choose hymns that expand on the healing themes raised in scripture and sermon.

As congregations initiate healing services, whether on Sunday morning or at specific times of the week, leaders must creatively integrate the emphasis on healing with every aspect of congregational life. In their commitment to embodying the reign of God, congregations are challenged to see healing worship and prayer as permeating and transforming the totality of their educational, administrative, evangelistic, and social outreach ministries.

CONTINUING HEALING EDUCATION

God's healing spirit breathes through the entire congregation, bringing new life and evoking the community's spiritual gifts. Within the body of Christ, there are many gifts and vocations. As the apostle Paul proclaims:

> Now there are varieties of gifts, but the same Spirit; and there are varieties of services, but the same Lord; and there are varieties of activities, but it is the same God who activates all of them in everyone. To each is given the manifestation of the Spirit for the common good. To one is given through the Spirit the

utterance of wisdom, and to another the utterance of knowledge according to the same Spirit, to another faith by the same Spirit, to another gifts of healing by the one Spirit, to another the working of miracles, to another prophecy, to another the discernment of spirits, to another various kinds of tongues, to another the interpretation of tongues. All these are activated by one and the same Spirit, who allots to each one individually just as the Spirit chooses. (1 Corinthians 12:4–11)

While I believe that each person can become a medium of God's healing touch, I also recognize that within the community of healers, there are many gifts and passions that emerge in the course of our adventures in spiritual growth. Within the body of Christ, there are the gifts of liturgical healing touch, worship leadership, listening and pastoral care, healing the dying, spiritual transformation, body work, preventative care, and complementary health care. Each of these gifts needs to be nurtured within a community of faith that provides theological education, spiritual guidance, ethical standards, and personal support. Since healing is a lifelong process in which each healing partner needs to commit her or himself to growth in healing and wholeness, congregations need to provide continuing education opportunities for participants in healing ministries. Programs in continuing education may be provided by congregations, clusters of congregations, seminaries, or regional denominational or ecumenical bodies. While there are many possible programmatic options in the adventure in healing and wholeness, I suggest the following areas of emphasis:

1. Adventures in theology, healing, and spiritual formation;

2. Listening and pastoral care;

3. Healing ethics;

4. Congregational health care and prevention;

5. Complementary health care and the church.

Adventures in theology, healing, and spiritual formation. Beyond the initial eight-week study group, it is important that members of healing teams explore Christian healing in the context of the whole ministry of the church as well as their own personal and spiritual growth. Periodically, courses should be offered in spirituality and spiritual formation, healing ministry, and Christian theology. These courses will equip these "healing partners" or "healing ministers" with the theological insight and spiritual maturity to respond to persons in need. As leaders of the healing ministry, they will have to address difficult theological questions with sensitivity and care. Courses of study might include:

1. Adventures in prayer and meditation;

2. Healing liturgies for the seasons of life;

3. An introduction to Christian theology.

Thankfully, there are many fine resources for courses that join theology, healing, and spirituality.[2]

Listening and pastoral care. Listening is at the heart of the healing process. In his own healing ministry, Jesus listened with the heart as well as the ears. In response to the pleas of a blind man, Jesus asks, "What do you want me to do for you?" Jesus did not force healing upon persons, but responded to their deepest spiritual, physical, emotional, and relational needs.

While healing partners do not need to be experts in mental health issues, they need to be sensitized to the psychological dynamics of health and illness, the nature of grief, and emotional responses to disability and terminal illness. Basic knowledge in these issues may prevent needless pain and suffering among persons who are already vulnerable as a result of their medical conditions. These courses may be offered in conjunction with Stephen Ministry and other congregational care programs or as part of a curriculum dedicated to healing and wholeness that would include seminars in:

1. The spirituality of aging;
2. Death and bereavement;
3. Spirituality and disability;
4. Mental health issues;
5. Medication and health.

These seminars integrate theological reflection, spiritual formation, and psychological insight with practical exercises in listening, open-ended questioning, and crisis care.

Healing ethics. Spiritual intimacy and healing touch are at the heart of congregational healing ministry. Since touch can harm as well as heal, healing partners must not only be screened through interviews and criminal background checks, they must also be trained in issues of appropriate touch, professional conduct, confidentiality, self-care, and personal ethics. It is essential for healing partners to affirm by their words, conduct, and silence that healing ministry is *always and only* for the benefit of the person in need. Accordingly, healing encounters must be grounded in self-awareness, intentionality, and a sense of appropriate boundaries. Given the proclivity of gossip in many congregations, training in confidentiality is absolutely necessary.

Training in healing ethics is not intended to be legalistic or imposed from without. Rather, it flows from a commitment to spiritual and ethical formation in which personal wholeness and self-care are joined with care for others. As healed healers, our commitment to our own healing process and the highest level of personal integrity is intimately related to our ability to share God's grace to persons in need.

Congregational health care and prevention. At the heart of an effective healing ministry is a commitment to prevention and well-being. Healing services are part of an ecology of health and healing that includes programs in blood pressure screening, diet, exercise, and stress reduction. God's aim at abundant life calls us to health promotion as well as prayerful response to illness. Members of the healing team may receive training in the essentials of congregational health ministry, including both prevention and advocacy. Ideally, healing teams should include health care professionals who can provide guidance in responding to persons responding to health crises. Seminars in prevention and congregational health care may include:

1. The essentials of a healthy lifestyle;

2. Exercise and fitness for senior adults;

3. Hospital visitation;

4. Health promotion in congregational life;

5. CPR (cardiopulmonary resuscitation);

6. Identifying risk factors.

After taking these seminars, healing partners will be equipped to provide workshops for the broader public under the overall direction of a physician or parish nurse.

Complementary health care and the church. The growing interest in complementary medicine challenges the church to become a leader in educating training persons in those complementary health modalities, appropriate to mainstream and progressive Christianity. Although these modalities are no substitute for the rituals of laying of hands and anointing with oil or the intercessory prayer ministry of the church, complementary health practices enhance overall wellness, provide pain relief and comfort for persons with chronic and life-threatening illnesses, and enhance immune system functioning.

As in the case of every other ministry of the church, the church's wellness ministry must aspire toward excellence in training and education, including the theological and spiritual foundations of complementary medicine and the ethics of healing partnerships. At the heart of the church's complementary health ministry is the affirmation that wherever truth and healing are present, God is its source. Congregational training in complementary medicine will include not only hands-on training in practices such as reiki and healing touch, but also emphases on the healing ministry of Jesus, Christian understandings of health and illness, Christian prayer and meditation, pastoral care and listening, and healthy touch. Congregational complementary health ministries should be linked to the healings of Jesus and to liturgical healing services in order to build bridges between faith, complementary medicine, and Western technological medicine.

HEALING MEDITATIONS FOR STUDY GROUPS

In the following paragraphs, I describe Christian spiritual practices that embrace both tradition and novelty. The use of spiritual disciplines is at the heart of congregational health ministry and healing worship.

Lectio divina. Dating back to the fourth century monastic Benedict of Narsia, Christians have read scripture in imaginative and transforming ways. The practice of *lectio divina* reminds us that God is still speaking in the words of scripture. We can experience God's presence in scripture in ways that transcend issues of language and world view. *Lectio divina* allows each person to have an intimate relationship with scripture. Though this intimate encounter with scripture needs to be complemented by the wisdom of the community of faith and the skills of biblical scholars, fresh encounters with scripture enable us to discover God's fidelity in the ever-changing moments of our personal and corporate histories. *Lectio divina,* or holy reading, engages the text, whether individually or in groups though the following steps:

1. The reading of a biblical passage two or three times with generous pauses;

2. Quiet meditation on the scripture;

3. Reflection on a word, image, or phrase that comes to your attention;

4. Reflection on the meaning of the word, image, or phrase for your life today;

5. Prayerful openness to how the word, image, or phrase might be embodied in your life;

6. Generous time for personal meditation on the word.

If *lectio divina* is done in a group setting, members should be invited to share their insights without judgment or critique. The group is called to listen to God's word in the words of each of their companions.

Centering prayer. While there is no clear origin of the practice of centering prayer, contemporary Christians have adopted this gentle form of meditative prayer in response to the growing interest in Buddhist and Hindu meditative practices, and most especially Transcendental Meditation.[3] Easily learned, centering prayer moves from focusing on a prayer word (or mantra) to experiencing God's "sighs too deep for words." Gentle in approach, centering prayer accepts the mind's distractions without judgment and then returns to our spiritual focus. Centering prayer is practiced in the following way:

1. A moment of quiet preparation;

2. Prayer for God's presence;

3. Focus on a prayer word (such as "love," "light," "healing," "peace," "Jesus");

4. If the mind is distracted, simply bring attention back to the prayer word without blame or judgment;

5. Concluding prayer.

While there is no legalistic time frame for the centering prayer, I would suggest minimally ten to twenty minutes twice daily.

Breath prayer. The practice of breath prayer is similar to that of centering prayer. One may simply sit a comfortable place and prayerfully inhale the spirit of God with each breath. When distractions or interruptions occur, one simply returns prayerfully to the breath without judgment or criticism. Often in my use of breath prayer, I invoke the words, "I breathe the spirit deeply in," as I inhale, and send that spirit out into the world as I exhale. Similar to centering prayer, breath prayer is most effective when practiced for ten to twenty minutes twice a day. In addition, whenever I begin to feel stress or anxiety, I take a moment simply to breathe in God's spirit and allow God to center and guide me once more.

Meditation on healing light. Light has always been a symbol of the divine. The divine light is described in terms of haloes surrounding the heads of Jesus, Mary, and the saints as well as the energy emanating from healing hands. In this meditation, one simply begins by breathing in the peace and presence of God. After a few minutes of relaxed breathing, image divine healing light entering your body with each breath. With every exhaling, send your light out into the world. Experience the light permeating and transforming every part of your body, beginning with the head and moving downward to the soles of the feet. If there are places where your personal energy seems blocked or where you are experiencing pain or discomfort, focus God's healing light on these parts of your body. After you have reached the soles of your feet, image the healing light surrounding your body with divine protection.

Healing light intercession. In John's prologue, the author proclaims that "the true light [the Logos or Christ], which enlightens everyone, was coming into the world" (John 1:9). Jesus affirms, "You are the light of the world" (Matthew 5:14). Our task as Christians is to bring forth the light in one another as we discover God's light in the most unlikely places.

In this meditation, begin with the light meditation described in the previous section. After you have completed the light meditation, begin to reflect on persons in your life. As you imagine each person, exhale God's light a few times and envisage it surrounding the one for whom you pray. Experience God's light bringing healing and wholeness to their lives. Repeat this light meditation for those persons for whom you are interceding.

You may also imaginatively breathe God's healing light to embrace and transform relationships, life events, situations, and corporate entities such as churches and nations. In envisaging persons as healed through God's light, we become partners in God's ever-present and non-local aim at healing.

Body of Christ meditation. This meditation is grounded in an imaginative encounter with the Paul's image of the body of Christ (1 Corinthians 12). As we experience this meditation, we are reminded of the interplay of our personal gifts and graces and our intimate relationships with our partners in the healing journey.

After a period of silence, the leader reads 1 Corinthians 12 in its entirety, reminding group members to remember their unique gifts and the role of the community in living out their gifts.

Take a moment to imagine yourself as a part of a vibrant, healthy, loving body. What does the body look like? What does it feel like to be part of such an energetic body? . . .

As you ponder this healthy body, imaginatively image your unique "part" in the body of Christ—what part of your body are you? What does your part look like? What role does your part have in the body? What supports the expression of your unique and special gifts? What stands in the way of your experiencing the fullness of your gifts? Take some time to reflect on this challenge. . . .

Now look around at the body as a whole. What parts of the body are most supportive of you? Are these parts representative of any persons in your life? Take time to give thanks for the parts of the body that support you and the

Giver of the gifts. . . .

In your gratitude, experience the joyful interplay of giving and receiving within this lively and inspired body. Feel God's holy energy flowing through your life and into the lives of your companions within this holy body. . . .

Conclude with a quiet prayer of gratitude for your gifts, for those who support your giftedness, and for the energy of love that flows through the body. . . .

Meditation on healing the planet. This guided meditation invites persons to visualize the relationship between their own wholeness and spiritual commitments and the healing of the planet.

Begin in quiet prayer, observing your breath, inhaling and exhaling. Experience yourself within the deep peace of God. As you gently breathe, reflect on the intricate connectedness of life—what realities shape your life? What brings health and wholeness to your life? What do you depend upon for your living and being? . . .

Take a moment to image those realities that threaten your well-being and their negative impact on your life. . . .

Now in the quiet, take a moment to pray for those positive and negative factors of life. As you continue in an attitude of contemplative prayer, image God's healing touch transforming your body, mind, and spirit. Image God's healing touch transforming your family—spouse, partner, parents, children, etc. Continue to image God's touch now transforming your workplace . . . congregation . . . neighborhood . . . city . . . nation . . . a country at war with your nation . . . and finally the whole earth. Experience the whole world cradled safely in God's hands as you feel your connectedness with all things. . . .

Now experience the circle of touch moving from the
whole back to the parts . . . the planet . . . a country at
war with your nation . . . your nation . . . city . . . neighborhood . . . workplace . . . congregation . . . family . . .
and back to yourself. Conclude with a prayer of intercession for the world and thanksgiving for the wonder of
life. Commit yourself to being a partner in God's aim at
healing the earth. . . .

Meditation on "the storm at sea."[4] The healed healer is challenged to be a "non-anxious presence" in her or his response to
persons in pain. Authentic empathy arises from the experience
of God's center within our personal center. We cultivate the
experience of our spiritual center through practices that remind
us of our essential wholeness and safety in companionship with
God. This meditation is intended to nurture a quiet center within the storms of life.

Begin by reading reflectively the words from Luke 8:22–25
with an awareness of the storms in your life. What do
these words say to you today? . . .

In the quiet, imagine a beautiful sunny day. You and a
number of your best friends are taking a voyage across a
lovely lake. You are celebrating your recent success as a
spiritual group. Imagine the scene as you gently glide
across the lake. Who is traveling with you? Take a
moment to visualize the faces of your closest companions.
What food and drink do you bring with you to celebrate
your success? . . .

Suddenly, in the midst of the celebration, you notice a
bolt of lightning across the sky and the crash of thunder.
The sky darkens and the wind picks up until it becomes
gale force. Your boat is now being buffeted about like a
child's toy. How do you feel as the storm tosses your boat
to and fro? . . .

In the midst of the storm, take a moment to listen to your own life. What storms are currently buffeting your life? How do you feel in the midst of these personal storms? What resources, if any, do you have to face the storms of your life? . . .

As the storm rages you cry out for God, forgetting that Jesus is with you. Suddenly, you remember that you are not alone—you remember that Jesus is with you. How do you feel to remember that the Healer is in your midst even in the storm? How does the perception of the storm change with the recognition of Jesus' presence? . . .

Suddenly, Jesus is standing beside you and speaks to the storm, "Peace, be still." Slowly, the sky lightens, the sea calms, and the storm recedes in the distance. All is well. Your boat gently glides to the other side of the lake and you joyfully disembark, ready for your next adventure. . . .

Take a moment to claim the positive emotions that were evoked by your discovery that God is with you in the storm. Take a moment to affirm your desire to remember Jesus in all of life's storms. . . .

As you emerge from this time of imaginative prayer, take a moment to thank God for God's presence and care in all the storms of life. . . .

chapter seven

Beyond the Cure, There is a Healing

But Mary stood weeping outside the tomb. As she wept, she bent over to look into the tomb; and she saw two angels in white, sitting where the body of Jesus had been lying, one at the head and the other at the feet. They said to her, "Woman, why are you weeping?" She said to them, "They have taken away my Lord, and I do not know where they have laid him." When she had said this, she turned around and saw Jesus standing there, but she did not know that it was Jesus. Jesus said to her, "Woman, why are you weeping? Whom are you looking for?" Supposing him to be the gardener, she said to him, "Sir, if you have carried him away, tell me where you have laid him, and I will take him away." Jesus said to her, "Mary!" She turned and said to him in Hebrew, "Rabbouni!" (which means Teacher). (John 20:11–16)

Over her many years as a pastor, Susan Frey has been the spiritual companion to many dying persons. In the course of her spiritual care, she has experienced many of her parishioners living through what Elizabeth Kubler Ross has described as the stages of dying. While some persons remain stuck in anger and denial, Pastor Frey has found that most persons of faith eventually discover a sense of peace in companionship with the God of Living and Dying. This peace which passes all understanding is often hard-won, but it is always life-changing.

Deeply spiritual, Martha believed that she could conquer the ovarian cancer with which she was diagnosed. The day after the diagnosis, she embarked on a path of spiritual and physical healing—visualization exercises, yoga, daily meditation, acupuncture and reiki healing touch, and positive affirmations. She surrounded herself with loved ones and made amends with those she felt she had injured in the course of sixty years. "I know that I will be healed," she shared with Pastor Frey, "My husband needs me and I want to live long enough to see the birth of my first grandchild. There is so much to live for. I can't die now!" At first, Martha's condition improved. Tests initially showed that her regimen of chemotherapy, complementary medicine, and spiritual discipline was working. Martha rejoiced, and thanked God for her anticipated cure. But, six months later, her condition reached a plateau. From then on, she battled just to remain stable.

As her condition slowly deteriorated and the harsh reality of death confronted her, Martha stepped up her commitment to physical and spiritual renewal. She gathered a prayer team of hundreds of persons throughout the country and attended every healing workshop in the area in addition to her congregation's weekly healing service. She even sought out faith healers whose theology or worship style radically differed from her own. She confessed, "During their sermons, I surrounded myself in healing light as a way of shutting out their simplistic theology. But, I know there is a power in their services and I will try anything to experience God's healing." Still, however, nothing changed.

One afternoon, Pastor Frey's sermon preparation was interrupted by a quiet knock at her study door. She greeted Martha who appeared physically haggard, but spiritually calm. After sharing stories about their families and about the upcoming birth of Martha's first grandchild, Martha closed her eyes for a few moments and then surprised Pastor Frey by her next words, "Susan, I think I've received the healing I've been praying for." After pausing to let the significance of her words sink in,

Martha continued, "Yes, I think I've received a healing, but not exactly the one I was looking for when I first heard I had cancer. Now, I know I am dying, and I can't do anything about that. But, I feel at peace. I tried so hard for a cure, but now I realize I needed something more than just a physical cure—I needed to know that God's love never ends, and now I do! Whether I die tomorrow or in twenty years, God will be with me every step of the way."

Over the next few months, Pastor Frey was Martha's faithful healing companion in the slow and often painful journey toward death. In the last week of her life, Martha gathered her closest friends for a final healing service. After the anointing and laying on of hands, Martha gently shared her heart with those she loved, "This has been a long tough journey, but I have been blessed. I have discovered that God is with me when all else fails. I have seen my granddaughter's smile. I am so grateful. But, I still wish I could see her grow into a young woman." After a few minutes of reflective silence, Martha chuckled and continued, "Perhaps I will see her after all, from a God's-eye view!" A few days later, Martha began a new adventure with God as her Holy Companion. She discovered that when there cannot be a cure, there can always be a healing.

HEALING THE DYING

For many years, I have told my medical students, "Every last one of your patients is going to die. Just hope it isn't on your watch!" I give this same advice to seminarians and recent graduates in their first ministerial call. Despite advances in Western technological medicine, the growing interplay of spirituality and medicine, and the increased use of complementary medicine, the mortality rate remains constant at 100%. Indeed, the fact that every person Jesus cured eventually died led C.S. Lewis to wonder if Jesus did Lazarus, Mary, and Martha any favors—after all, he had to die twice!

In recognizing the universality of death, Martin Luther asserted that in the midst of life, we are surrounded by death. The reality of death can be overwhelming, painful, and heartbreaking. The cost of loving another person deeply is eventually "saying goodbye" to your beloved and living on without her or him. Those who are dying must give up the familiar world of this good and beautiful earth. While there may be glorious sunrises and sunsets and happy reunions in God's Everlasting Realm, we must let go of our beloved's touch, the changing seasons, and the wonder of our own planet's sunrise and sunset in order to embrace the Heavenly Realm. But, with the hope of one who has walked through life's darkest valleys and discovered God's presence there, Luther also affirmed, in the midst of death, we are surrounded by life.

While death is seldom painless, I believe that when there cannot be a cure, there can always be a healing. We can experience God's peace even as we walk through the valley of the shadow of death.

Still, death is the greatest challenge to our hopes for healing and wholeness. At first glance, death is the ultimate defeat of our prayers. But, confronting our mortality may change our expectations of God and our hopes for the future. Tony confessed that he didn't know what to pray for as he faced the death of his life-long companion Michael with whom he had traveled a long and circuitous journey with AIDS. "For the past few years, I've prayed for a cure. But, now I don't see that happening. Can I pray for a peaceful death? There are times I feel guilty and, as a former Pentecostal, I wonder if I'm letting God down by not claiming a physical healing. But I just want him to find peace and comfort in his final days." In such moments, a healing pastor integrates her best theological insights along with pastoral sensitivity and spiritual care. When the rhythm of conversation moves from addressing feelings of grief and loss to God's will and the hope for eternal life, the sensitive pastor is confronted with his own questions and doubts and his desire to say a healing word about God and the future. He must confront his own attitudes toward illness and death in order to be a "healed healer" for those at life's descending edges.

From time to time, I hear reports—mostly from televangelists —about people being raised from the dead or growing new arms or legs. While there may very well be, as C.S. Lewis notes, spiritual and physical laws that transcend our current scientific and spiritual understanding of reality, there seems to be a point in life when not even the prayers of the faithful or the love of God can cure the dying. Indeed, the trustworthiness of God depends on a cosmic and cellular predictability that even God chooses not to transgress. There is a time and season for everything, and death and grief are natural seasons in every life. We must admit that once a person has reached a certain health condition—final stage cancer or AIDS, or flat EEG—the appropriate spiritual response is to pray for a peaceful and healing death rather than a physical cure or restoration.

To pray for a spiritual healing rather a physical cure is not to limit God's power, but to affirm that death may be the pathway to God's ultimate healing. God's power is revealed in abiding companionship and eternal love and not arbitrary and coercive interventions in matters of life and death. We all must eventually die. Our faith is that the One who loved us into life will receive us lovingly at the hour of our death and guide us toward new adventures of creativity and love.

Death confronts us with our limitations as mortals. Our spiritual practices cannot insure that our lives will be free from debilitating pain, the realities of aging, chronic illness, and eventually death. The apostle Paul's own spiritual struggles remind us that there is no one-to-one correspondence between faith and health. For years, he was tormented by a chronic ailment, "a thorn in the flesh." Neither his prayers nor mystical experiences could restore him to health and well-being. Perhaps, the apostle might have wondered if God were punishing him for his youthful persecution of the first Christians. He may have internalized the punitive and guilt-producing theology of his pre-Christian days. Although the apostle never received a physical cure, he rejoiced that he had experienced God's healing touch. "Three times I appealed to [God] about this, that it would leave me, but [God] said to me, 'My grace is sufficient for you, for power is made perfect in weakness'" (2 Corinthians 12:8–9). Paul experienced a life-changing healing, despite the fact that he was never cured.

At the descending edges of life or as we face chronic debilitation, we must depend entirely on the grace of God and a supportive community of faith to remind us that we are never alone in life and death. Healing worship provides physical transformation for some persons, but also comfort and peace for those who may never get well. According to some Christian mystics, "God is the circle, whose center is everywhere, and whose circumference is nowhere." Healing worship and pastoral care remind us that we are always in the circle of God's love, regardless of our physical, mental, or spiritual condition.

THE CIRCLE OF HEALING

Healing ministry affirms God's abundant life amid the stark realities of death and dying. As pastors and church leaders, our calling is to mediate God's healing touch to dying persons through creative and sensitive pastoral care, spiritual formation, theological reflection, and liturgical worship. Healing worship is the center of a circle that brings health and wholeness to persons at every condition of life. In the following paragraphs, I will reflect briefly on how we can support spiritual healing among dying persons. Within this healing circle, theology, spiritual formation, worship, and pastoral care are woven together in order to bring healing and wholeness to those who may never get well.

Pastoral care for dying persons. The first movement in our response to persons diagnosed with life-threatening and terminal illnesses is pastoral care. The healing pastor has no expectations or preconceptions regarding the course the healing process will take. She simply takes those who are dying as they are without judgment or the urge to alter their experience in any way. He recognizes that healing comes through accepting the whole range of a person's emotional experience, rather than denying life's darkest moments. With theologian Nelle Morton, we are called simply to listen one another into speech. The ministry of prayerful listening is a profound act of trust in God's presence in each person's personal experience and spiritual journey.

In the months following his diagnosis with pancreatic cancer, Stephen moved from denial and anger to creative acceptance of his mortality as a result of his weekly conversations with his pastor. Stephen noted, "Jim didn't say much. But, his study was always a safe place for me to share my terror and rage. He never judged or denied what I was feeling. His listening spirit enabled me to live with my cancer and find creative ways to love my family despite my physical condition. His words never got in the way. Sure, we talked theology, and prayed together, but only at my request."

Healing care is not only a matter of listening and accepting, but also involves faithful companionship. When death is all around us, we need healing companions who will never forsake us. These companions walk the walk, and become, to use Luther's words, "little Christs" as we face our journey into unknown lands.

Our congregations are called to be houses of hope and healing, not just on Sunday morning or at healing services, but in every aspect of their ministries. In our companionship with the dying, we become God's "real presence," reminding them that they are never alone. Accordingly, we need to prepare for our response to dying persons by facing our own fears and doubts. Our own self-awareness and self-acceptance enable us to embrace the full range of another's response to the reality of death. In our openness to the fullness of experience, those who have been diagnosed with terminal illness become God's "real presence" to the currently healthy, reminding them that God seeks healing even in our dying process.

Spiritual transformation for dying persons. Each moment of experience integrates birthing and dying. In order to embrace every new moment, we must let go of the immediacy of the most recent moment. But, the past provides the energy and direction from which the present moment arises. Spiritual growth occurs when we open ourselves to God's wisdom, companionship, and guidance in each moment of birthing and dying. The dying are still living, and just as capable of hearing God's "sighs too deep for words" as those who envisage themselves as being alive in 2050. While there are no specific "arts of dying" for twenty-first century persons, the paths of prayer, meditation, imagination, and *lectio divina* provide guidance at every stage of life.[1]

In Madeleine L'Engle's novel *The Ring of Endless Light*, Vicky Austin's grandfather, dying of acute leukemia after a long and adventurous life, notes that in his current physical condition, his calling is simply to pray for the world. While serious illness often constricts our vision of reality and concern for others, prayer connects us with the totality of life as a divine-human adventure. For those who have received good pastoral care and are now able to look beyond their own pain, prayers of petition, intercession, and thanksgiving enlarge their spiritual stature and contribute to the healing of the world. Spiritual peace is the gift of experiencing our own lives as part of a larger personal and cosmic journey in which we share in the health and wholeness of the family, community, and planet. Healing pastors not only pray for the sick, but invite the sick to become God's partners in bringing wholeness to a world they may never see. As recent medical studies suggest, our prayers make a difference to those for whom we pray. The intercessions of the dying may the "tipping point" between health and illness, and spiritual life and death, for our families, congregations, communities, and planet.

Meditative prayer has been found to calm spirit, mind, and body. Times of quiet centering root us in divine companionship and open us to the healing energy available for us in the present moment. Although meditative prayer may not significantly increase the lifespan of dying persons, it eases the pain by placing their physical ailments within the context of a larger sense of peace.

In my own ministry, I often teach persons to join meditation and centering prayer with chemotherapy treatments. In quiet centering, they find a peace that calms anxiety and reduces pain. In this same spirit, guided healing visualizations remind persons that Christ is their constant companion in life's most difficult situations. To envisage Christ greeting them in their final moments brings peace, hope, and courage to persons facing their imminent deaths. I also believe that complementary health practices such as reiki, healing touch, acupuncture, and therapeutic touch bring pain relief and a greater sense of personal control amid processes that cannot be controlled by acts of will or medical intervention.

Joining spiritual formation with pastoral care enables persons with life-threatening illnesses to experience their lives as *lectio divina*, or a holy revelation of God. Just as they might look at a scripture passage for God's guidance through a word or image, they are invited to interpret their lives in all their complexity and struggle as encounters with God and revelations of God's presence. Wisdom can be found in every life situation for those who believe that God is our ever-present guide and companion. Death can teach us to "number our days" and treat each moment as a holy adventure in love and thanksgiving.

Theology at the edges of life. While theology is foundational to spiritual formation, pastoral care, and worship, in the movement of healing ministry theological reflection is often the last step in the process of facing death and dying. A holistic faith embraces the rawness of our emotions as a prelude to theological reflection, especially for persons who tend to deny their emotional lives. It embraces despair and doubt as pathways to healing and wholeness. Still, theological issues will eventually emerge in every long-term pastoral relationship. Nowhere is the quest for meaning greater than in the months following the diagnosis of a life-threatening or incurable illness. We ponder "why" this is happening to us. We may wonder if we are being punished for previous misdeeds or are victims of the inscrutable will of an all-powerful God. We may question the choices we have made and the life we have lived as well as search for something of value we can pass on to the next generation.

In caring for the dying, the sensitive pastor raises theological issues in a gentle and non-coercive way. Trusting that God's grace, and not our own personal orthodoxy, is the source of healing and salvation, the pastor recognizes that "we see in a mirror, dimly" (1 Corinthians 13:112a) and that the likelihood of death may often muddle, rather than clarify, a person's theological beliefs.

Still, I believe the pastor can dialogically share healthy and comforting theological images with dying persons. Such thin places in the spiritual journey call the pastor to discover her or his own healing theological affirmations as a means to nurturing open-ended conversations when theological questions arise. As I respond to persons with life-threatening illnesses, I seek to share quietly and, at times, indirectly the faith I affirm with the recognition that those with whom I speak need to internalize these truths in their own unique ways. I welcome their anger, doubt, and sense of meaninglessness as essential aspects of the healing process. Healing must embrace the emotions as well as the intellect and imagination.

First, I remind persons facing death of the reality of God's presence, especially in those "god-forsaken" moments of life. I believe that God is our companion in living and dying. As the apostle Paul proclaims, nothing can "separate us from the love of God in Christ Jesus our Lord" (Romans 8:38–39). God is faithful and God will complete God's work in our lives as a prelude to God's everlasting adventure beyond the grave.

Second, I invite persons confronting their mortality to reflect upon their unique vocation at this point in their lives. The omnipresent God is constantly inviting us to grow spiritually, intellectually, emotionally, and relationally. Even at life's descending edges, God's holy desire still calls us to new understandings of our lives and new behaviors in relationship with others. Spiritual healing is the gift of God's holy adventure at any moment of life. We can be transformed and change our lives when we respond to God's healing presence. Our dying process can be a witness to our faithfulness to God and our love for others. When we discover our vocation or calling, we experience greater meaning, empowerment, and purpose in any condition of life. Our lives become our gifts to God, our communities, and our families.

Third, I ask my companions in the dying process to ponder their vision of survival after death. While the hope for everlasting life does not deny the harsh realities of grief, loss, and death, trusting the future in God's care enables us to live creatively and openly in the present. Death may end one journey, but it may also be the open door for a new and surprising partnership with God.

As I ponder the question of immortality, I recognize two aspects of our experience of eternal life. The first is God's preservation of the goodness and beauty of our lives. What we do matters eternally because God preserves all that is good in ourselves and those we love. While we may forget our own identity, God never forgets our lives and loves.

The second aspect is our holy adventure beyond the grave. The growing interest in "near death experiences" confirms the insights of biblical spirituality. Although their interpretations of immortality may differ, biblically spirituality and the accounts of near death experiences both point to life after death as profoundly relational, healing, and adventurous. Our physical death does not mark the end of our lives, but the beginning of a new spiritual adventure in which the obstructions to our spiritual growth are removed. Beyond the grave, I believe that we continue to grow in wisdom, stature, and love. In the afterlife, we have opportunities to continue relationships and make amends with those we have hurt as we grow in grace and beauty. Theological imagination invites us to image new and abundant life with God as our companion and teacher. Born into loving arms, we anticipate the loving arms that will greet us as we take our last breath. The creative energy of life continues beyond the grave and propels us toward our destiny as God's beloved children.

Worship with the dying. The calling of the church is to heal the living and dying with the recognition that, despite their prognosis, the dying are still alive! Indeed, our healing ministries recognize the wisdom of a plaque at the College of Surgeons at Paris, "We are the dying taking care of the dying." Accordingly, persons diagnosed with terminal illnesses have an essential place at our healing services. They are not signs of spiritual failure, divine apathy, or lack of faith, but witnesses to God's healing of the spirit as well as the flesh. Regardless of our physical condition, we need God's healing touch. In fact, the only difference between the physically healthy and those diagnosed with terminal illnesses is the clarity with which we recognize and struggle with our mortality. Perhaps, the only prayer we need to make is "God heal me and those I love" as we leave the rest to God's intimate and infinite wisdom.

Although it is appropriate to have individual healing services and healing prayers for persons who are unable to leave home, it is still important for those who are able to join the healing community in prayer and thanksgiving. The prayers of a faithful community sustain and inspire those who are walking in the valley of the shadow of death. Our prayers and physical presence as a community releases a healing energy that eases physical pain and provides a sense of spiritual wholeness. At certain times, it may even be appropriate for a community of healing partners to create a healing circle at the home of one who is no longer able to travel to the healing service. In the interplay of solitude and community, we discover that we are always joined with the body of Christ.

With boldness, we can pray that God's healing touch rest upon persons in every physical condition. This is not denial, but the affirmation that we all need healing all of the time, and persons diagnosed with terminal illness are no exception. God's love meets us wherever we are with the unique healing that we need in the here and now.

In our welcome of dying persons to healing services, we consciously face our own fears and overcome the cultural taboos that surround death and dying. We move from isolation and fear to love and community. Persons confronting their mortality contribute to the healing of faith communities by their faithful witness that God's love is stronger than death. The witness of their own healing adventure gives us confidence to place our own mortality in the hands of a loving God.

HEALING AT THE EDGES OF LIFE

In times of crisis, the faith of the community sustains us even when our own faith is shaken. We trust others to believe on our behalf until we can again believe for ourselves. Healing rituals create a protective circle of love for those who are beginning their final journey. In the spirit of the Celtic prayer of encircling, our prayers witness to a Love that encompasses us in every season of life. Within the healing circle, our prayers with the dying awaken a healing energy that enables us to experience wholeness as we face our greatest fears.[2]

Prayers with the dying. I conclude this book with prayerful affirmations for the dying and their families. They are meant to provide a healing path that you may adapt to the uniqueness of your own pastoral ministry and remind you that our endings, like our beginnings, are in the circle of God's love. A prayer in the Anglican tradition reminds the dying and their loved ones that God's holy adventure joins earthly and everlasting healing communities.

Deliver your servant _____, O Sovereign Lord Christ, from all evil, and set her [or him] free from every bond; that she [or he] may rest with all your saints in the eternal habitations; where with [the Creator] and the Holy Spirit, you live and reign, one God, forever and ever.[3]

At the moment when all life support systems are withdrawn, the community may pray for God's healing breath that joins time and eternity.

God of compassion and love,
you have breathed into us the breath of life
and have given us the exercise of our minds and will.
In our frailty, we surrender all life to you from whom it came,
through Jesus Christ our Lord. Amen.[4]

The United Church of Christ "prayer at the time of dying" seeks divine comfort and reassurance for the spiritual journey ahead.

Eternal God,
you know our needs before we ask,
and you hear our cries
through lips unable to speak.
Hear with compassion

the yearnings of your servant _____ ,
and the prayers that we would pray had we the words.
Grant her [or him] the assurance
of your embrace,
the ears of faith
to hear your voice,
and the eyes of hope to see your light.
Release her [or him] from all fear
and from the constraints of life's faults
that she [he] may breathe her [his] last
in the peace of your words:
Well done,
good and faithful servant;
enter into the joy of your God.
We ask this through Jesus Christ our Savior. Amen.[5]

At the hour of death, the recently bereaved struggle to find
meaning and hope in their grief. They, too, need to hear God's
word of grace and comfort amid their many, often contradicto-
ry, feelings.

Great God of all mystery,
if in the presence of death our thoughts are startled
and our words flutter about like frightened birds,
bring us stillness
that we may cover the sorrow of our hearts
with folded hands.
Give us grace to wait on you silently and with patience.
You are nearer to us than we know,
closer than we can imagine.
If we cannot find you,
it is because we search in far places.
Before we felt the pain,
you suffered it;
before the burden came upon us,

your strength lifted it;
before the sorrow darkened our hearts,
you were grieved.
As you walk in the valley of every shadow,
be our good shepherd
and sustain us while we walk with you,
lest in weakness we falter.
Though the pain deepens,
keep us in your way
and guide us past every danger;
through Jesus Christ our Savior. Amen.[6]

As we breathe our final breaths, the circle of healing love continues. The Divine Circle, "whose center is everywhere and whose circumference is nowhere," embraces, guides, and transforms. In life and in death, in dying and grieving, there are new adventures ahead in companionship with the Holy Adventure whose healing presence touches and makes whole. At every moment from birth to death, God calls our name and, like Mary of Magdala, we hear and are healed.

All-loving God,
Your love gave birth to the universe,
Your spirit gave birth to our lives.
Within your circle of love,
we have everlasting life.
Within your ever new Adventure,
we are called to new adventures.
Your blessing is upon _____
as she [or he] lets go of this life
to embrace the adventure that lies ahead.
Your blessing is upon us as we let go of _____
and enter our own holy adventures.
Your healing touch cleanses, transforms, and revives _____.
Your healing touch cleanses, transforms, and revives us.

God of loving adventure,
together we walk into an unknown future,
trusting that future to you,
knowing that the healing circle continues
in this world and in the adventure ahead.

With Christ as our everlasting companion,
we breathe your Loving Spirit
as we trust and let go. Amen.

Notes

CHAPTER ONE

1. The names and situations of persons whose healing stories are described in this book have been altered in order to protect their privacy and the privacy of their congregations.

2. The following books by physicians will be helpful in exploring the interplay of spirituality and medicine: Larry Dossey, *Healing Words: The Power of Prayer and the Practice of Medicine* (San Francisco: HarperSan Francisco, 1995); Harold G. Koenig, *Is Religion Good for Your Health?* (New York: Haworth, 1997) and *The Healing Power of Faith* (New York: Simon and Schuster, 1999); Dale A. Matthews and Connie Clark, *The Faith Factor: Proof of the Healing Power of Prayer* (New York: Viking, 1998).

3. Marcus Borg and N.T. Wright, *The Meaning of Jesus: Two Visions* (San Francisco: HarperSan Francisco, 2000); John P. Meier, *A Marginal Jew: Rethinking the Historical Jesus: Mentor, Message, and Miracles* (New York: Anchor Bible, 1994).

4. For a comprehensive catalogue of healing services from various Christian traditions, see Abigail Rian Evans,

Healing Liturgies for the Seasons of Life (Louisville: Westminster/John Knox, 2004). For in-depth studies on the healings of Jesus, see Bruce G. Epperly, *God's Touch: Faith, Wholeness, and the Healing Miracles of Jesus* (Louisville: Westminster/John Knox, 2001) and Morton T. Kelsey, *Healing and Christianity* (Minneapolis: Augsburg/Fortress, 1995).

5. Evans, *Healing Liturgies*, p. 1.

6. Ibid., p. xii.

7. For a discussion of new age understandings of the source of illness, see Bruce G. Epperly, *Crystal and Cross: Christians and New Age in Creative Dialogue* (Mystic, CT: Twenty Third Publications, 1996), pp. 97-128.

8. Wayne W. Dyer, *There is a Spiritual Solution to Every Problem* (New York: HarperCollins, 2001), p. 17.

9. Denise Dombkowski Hopkins, *Journey Through the Psalms*, rev. ed. (St. Louis: Chalice, 2002), p. 47-48.

10. Don E. Saliers, *Worship as Theology: Foretaste of Glory Divine* (Nashville: Abingdon, 1994), p. 15.

11. "Precious Lord, Take My Hand," Thomas Dorsey; "Healer of our Ev'ry

Ill," Mary Haugen; "He Touched
Me," William J. Gaither.
12. Evans, *Healing Liturgies*, p. 13.

CHAPTER TWO

1. Walter Brueggemann, *The
Prophetic Imagination* (Minneapolis:
Augsburg/Fortress, 2001).
2. While there are many fine
preaching texts, I have found the fol-
lowing quite helpful both in terms of
the theology and practice of preach-
ing: Clark M. Williamson and Ronald
J. Allen, *A Credible and Timely
Word: Process Theology and
Preaching* (St. Louis: Chalice, 1991);
Ronald J. Allen, *Preaching and
Practical Ministry* (St. Louis: Chalice,
1991); Frederick Buechner, *Telling the
Truth: The Gospel as Tragedy,
Comedy and Fairy Tale* (San
Francisco: HarperSan Francisco,
1977); Fred B. Craddock, *As One
Without Authority* (Nashville:
Abingdon, 1979); Marjorie Hewitt
Suchocki, *The Whispered Word: A
Theology of Preaching* (St. Louis:
Chalice, 1997); Barbara Brown
Taylor, *The Preaching Life* (New
York: Cowley, 1993).
3. Thich Nhat Hanh, *Peace Is Every
Step: The Path of Mindfulness in
Everyday Life* (New York: Bantam,
1992), pp. 8-11.
4. Herbert Benson, *Beyond the
Relaxation Response: How to Harness
the Healing Power of Your Personal
Beliefs* (New York: Times Books,
1984).
5. For contemporary versions of
Benedictine spirituality, see Kathleen
Norris, *Cloister Walk* (New York:
Riverhead, 1997) and Norvene Vest,
*Preferring Christ: A Devotional
Commentary on the Rule of St.
Benedict*(New York: Morehouse Press,
2004).

6. For a more detailed discussion of
the use of affirmations in spiritual formation, see Bruce G. Epperly, *The
Power of Affirmative Faith* (St. Louis:
Chalice Press, 2000).

CHAPTER THREE

1. For a discussion of reiki, see
Bruce G. Epperly and Katherine Gould
Epperly, *Reiki Healing Touch and the
Way of Jesus* (Kelowna, British
Columbia: Northstone, 2005).
2. See Bernie S. Siegel, *Love,
Medicine and Miracles* (New York:
Harper and Row, 1986) and O. Carl
Simonton, Stephanie Matthews
Simonton, and James Creighton,
Getting Well Again (Los Angeles: J.P.
Tarcher, 1978).
3. "To Forgive is Divine: The
Scientific Study of Forgiveness."
Annual Report: John Templeton
Foundation (Radnor, PA: John
Templeton Foundation, 2004).
4. United Church of Christ Office
for Church Life and Leadership, *Book
of Worship: United Church of Christ*
(New York: Office of Church Life and
Leadership, 1986), pp. 296-320;
Theology and Worship Ministry Unit
for the Presbyterian Church (USA) and
the Cumberland Presbyterian Church,
Book of Common Worship
(Louisville, KY: Westminster/John
Knox 1993), pp. 1005-1017.
5. UCC *Book of Worship*, p. 306.
6. Ibid., p. 307.
7. Ibid., p. 307.
8. Ibid., p. 310-311.
9. Presbyterian *Book of Common
Worship*, p. 1005.
10. Gary Gunderson, *Deeply Woven
Roots: Improving the Quality of Life
in Your Community* (Minneapolis:
Augsburg/Fortress, 1997).
11. Kenneth Pelletier, *Healthy People
in Unhealthy Places: Stress and Fitness*

at Work (New York: Doubleday, 1984).

12. Nelle Morton, *The Journey Is Home* (Boston: Beacon Press, 1985), p. 128.

13. Presbyterian *Book of Common Worship*, pp. 1006-1007.

14. Ibid., p. 1007.

15. UCC *Book of Worship*, p. 312.

16. Presbyterian *Book of Common Worship*, pp.1010-1011.

17. UCC *Book of Worship*, p.315.

18. Ibid., p. 317.

19. Presbyterian, *Book of Common Worship*, p. 1012.

20. UCC *Book of Worship*, p. 318-319.

21. Quoted in Matthew Fox, *Original Blessing: A Primer in Creation Spirituality* (Santa Fe, NM: Bear & Co., 1983), p.109.

22. UCC *Book of Worship*, p. 319-320.

CHAPTER FOUR

1. Olivier Clemént, *Taizé: A Meaning to Life* (Chicago: GIA Publications, 1997), p. 30.

2. Ibid., p. 38.

3. For a selection of Taizé chants, see Jacques Berthier, *Taizé: Songs For Prayer* (Chicago: GIA Publications, 1998).

4. Jacques Berthier, *Music from Taizé* (Chicago: GIA Productions, 1981), p. 100.

5. Berthier, *Songs for Prayer*, p. 25.

6. Ibid., p. 42.

7. Ibid., p. 40.

8. Ibid., p. 28.

9. Ibid., p. 6.

10. One can do this in one's imagination by simply drawing a circle with your finger or visualizing yourself dancing in a Celtic circle.

11. Adapted from *The Iona Community Worship Book* (Argyll,

Scotland: Wild Goose, 1991), p. 39.

12. Agnes Sanford, *Healing Light* (St. Paul, Macalester Park Publishing, 1978).

13. David J. Fleming, S.J., *The Spiritual Exercises of St. Ignatius: A Literal Translation and Contemporary Reading* (St. Louis: The Institute of Jesuit Sources, 1978).

14. Resources for imaginative prayer related to the healings of Jesus can be found in Bruce Epperly, *God's Touch*; Bruce Epperly, *Power of Affirmative Faith*; and Bruce Epperly and Katherine Epperly, *Reiki Healing Touch*. This imaginative prayer is adapted from *God's Touch*, p. 47-48.

15. Candace B. Pert, *The Molecules of Emotion: The Science Behind Mind-Body Medicine* (New York: Scribner, 1999).

16. For biblical affirmations, see Bruce Epperly, *Power of Affirmative Faith*.

17. Morton, *Journey Is Home*, p. 128.

18. There are many scriptures that inspire *lectio divina*: the woman with the flow of blood (Mark 5:25–34); the man who had been paralyzed thirty-eight years (John 5:4–19): the man born blind (John 9:1–7); the centurion's servant (Luke 7:1–10); the healing of Naaman (2 Kings 5:1–14).

19. Rita Nakashima Brock and Rebecca Ann Parker, *Proverbs of Ashes: Violence, Redemptive Suffering, and the Search for What Saves Us* (Boston: Beacon Press, 2001), p. 13.

20. This service is adapted from Bruce Epperly and Katherine Epperly, *Reiki Healing Touch*, p. 110-113. It was composed by Bruce Epperly and Anna Rollins for a retreat on Christian reiki held at Kirkridge Retreat and Conference Center, Bangor, Pennsylvania.

CHAPTER FIVE

1. Soren Kierkegaard, *Purity of Heart Is to Will One Thing* (New York: Harper and Brothers, 1948).

2. Abraham Joshua Heschel, *The Sabbath* (New York: Farrar, Strauss, and Giroux, 1988), p. 29.

3. Tilden Edwards, *Sabbath Time: Understanding and Practice for Contemporary Christians* (New York: Seabury Press, 1982), p. 31.

4. Heschel, *Sabbath*, p. 21.

5. Julie Denison, "Not Less But a Different Kind of Touch," *Christian Century* (February 21, 1991), p. 201.

6. Reiki is a form of still or healing touch that brings greater comfort, peace, and well-being to both giver and receiver. Reiki, or universal energy, balances and harmonizes our personal and communal energy, and is a prayerful form of laying on of hands. See www.ants.edu/academics/fhs/reiki.html for more information on the reiki program at Andover Newton Theological School. For information on the relationship between reiki and Christianity, see Bruce Epperly and Katherine Epperly, *Reiki Healing Touch* or contact bepperly@lancasterseminary.edu.

7. The New Standard Revised Version's alternative translation, "stature," better fits the meaning of this passage as it relates to Jesus' own spiritual growth.

CHAPTER SIX

1. Evans, *Healing Liturgies*, p. 4.

2. Helpful texts include: Bruce Epperly, *God's Touch* and *Power of Affirmative Faith*; Kelsey, *Healing and Christianity*; Tilda Norberg and Robert D. Webber, *Stretch Out Your Hand*, rev. ed. (Nashville: Upper Room, 1999); James K. Wagner, *An Adventure in Healing and Wholeness: The Healing Ministry of Christ in the Church Today* (Nashville: Upper Room, 1993).

3. M. Basil Pennington, *The Way Back Home: An Introduction to Centerine Prayer* (New York: Paulist Press, 1989).

4. Bruce Epperly, *Power of Affirmative Faith*, p. 48-49.

CHAPTER SEVEN

1. For a more detailed discussion on contemporary arts of dying, see Bruce G. Epperly and Lewis D. Solomon, *Finding Angels in Boulders: An Interfaith Discussion on Dying and Death* (St. Louis: Chalice, 2004).

2. For more complete examples of prayers at life's edges, see UCC *Book of Worship*, "Order of Healing for Use with an Individual," pp. 296-305, "Order of Worship for the Time of Dying," pp. 359-366; and Evans, *Healing Liturgies*, for persons with AIDS, pp. 263-276; for persons with cancer or stroke, pp. 277-284; prayers related to death and dying, pp. 287-306; prayers for the families of the dying, pp. 307-311.

3. Evans, *Healing Liturgies*, p. 295.

4. Ibid., pp. 296-297.

5. UCC *Book of Worship*, p. 362.

6. Ibid., pp. 364-365.